Emerging Leadership

LEADING OTHERS:
SHARING FAITH

Stanley E. Granberg

Contents

Letter of Welcome

Dear Emerging Leader,

Welcome to the Emerging Leader Training (ELT) series, module 2. If you come to this module having completed the *Spiritual Formation* module, you have spent time exploring your unique personality, your life experiences, and the spiritual giftedness God has provided you. You've also been leading a prayer team that has been earnestly praying for you and your development as a godly leader. Now you are ready to engage in the spiritual discipline of sharing faith.

Sharing faith is perhaps the most dynamic (and intimidating) activity that you as a godly leader will do. I find the process of sharing faith with those who are not yet Jesus followers one of the most delightful things I do. When you engage people in spiritual conversations, they allow you to share with them, at least for the moment, in their unique life journey. This is truly the cutting edge of God's kingdom work, where new faith is born and God's rule breaks into life.

By choosing to participate in the Kairos Emerging Leader Training series, you are saying you are serious about your development as a godly leader. You are asking those around you—your missional director, your church leaders, and significant people in your church body—to guide, instruct, help and encourage you. You are placing yourself in God's hands, allowing him to mold you through the set of experiences provided in the ELT series so you can become the leader he intends for you to be.

The mission of Kairos Church Planting is to see a generation of 21st century churches planted across America. These new churches will need a variety of godly leaders: lead church planters, worship leaders, prayer leaders, missional community leaders, and committed Christians who know how to live a missional, kingdom lifestyle. I believe you are one of these new leaders. The Kairos Emerging Leader Training series was written to provide you a structured, hands-on way to develop into a dynamic 21st century leader.

God bless you fully in your developing journey. Listen closely for his word to you. Open your heart to his heart. Let God's passions become yours.

I look forward to meeting you one day, if not here, then in God's eternal future as together we stand surrounded by the multitude, praising God for finding us, his lost people.

In the love and power of the risen Lord,

Stan Granberg, PhD
Kairos Executive Director

Self-Study Schedule and Exercise List

This module provides you guided exercises to train you to become a disciple who knows how to effectively share faith. Use this schedule to plan your progress. Begin each lesson by reading the book chapters. The core exercises are what you will do to develop the faith sharing skills that characterize a godly leader. Record your response to the core exercises in your personal answer book. If you return the answer book to Kairos, we will send you a certificate of completion. This module is designed to take six months to complete. Look over your personal calendar and enter your expected completion date for each core exercise.

Unit	Lesson	Readings	Core Exercises	Date to Complete
	1 - About This Module		Missional Director Meeting #1	
A - Starting Points	2 - Assessing Your Evangelism 3 - Seeing God's Lost People	Hybels Chapters 1-4	60-second Faith Statement Kairos Evangelism Assessment Restaurant Praying	
B - Understanding Unbelief	4 - Who Are God's Lost People 5 - Why People Don't Believe	Hybels Chapters 5-9	Missional Director Meeting #2 3 Question Conversation Prayer Focus List Spiritual Diagnosis	
C - Conversion	6 - Understanding Conversion 7 - Helping People Towards Conversion	Hybels Chapters 10-15	Your Personal Conversion Story Your Spiritual Journey Guide	
D - Connecting With God's Lost People	8 - Servant Evangelism 9 - Extending Invitations	Poole Introduction-Chapter 4	Missional Director Meeting #3 Conversation - What Do People Think About God? Assemble Your Team	
E - Creating Seeker Groups	10 - Coming to Faith in Community 11 - Your Seeker Group Meetings	Poole Chapters 5-10	Gather Seekers Funnel of Consideration Missional Director Meeting #4	
F - Strategy Assignment	12 - Conduct a Seeker Group		Planning Your Seeker Groups Seeker Meetings Follow-Up Missional Director Meeting #5	

The Emerging Leader Training Process

Background

The Emerging Leader Training (ELT) series is a product of Kairos Church Planting. The ELT is designed as a guided development process to engage emerging Christian leaders in leadership tasks that will grow their missional leadership skills. We have several purposes in providing the ELT:

- To provide emerging leaders with a guided process of personal development as a godly leader.

- To give planting churches a tool to raise up leaders and new church planters from their members.

- To give new churches a tool for training future staff ministers, team leaders, apprentices, and church planters.

- To provide those who have gone through a planter assessment with a process for developing skills they may still need to be ready to lead or be on a new church plant team.

ELT Content

The ELT series contains four modules spaced across two years. Year one modules cover basic leadership: 1) *Spiritual Formation* and 2) *Sharing Faith*. Year two covers leadership skills more intentionally focused on church planting through 3) *Essential Leadership* and 4) *Leading by Design*.

The modules are keyed to leadership skills assessed in the Emerging Leadership Initiative's Initial Screening Assessment (ISA), a skills inventory created to identify potential church planters. These skills are important skills for anyone who wishes to be a leader in 21st century churches. Sixty-eight of the eighty-five components measured in the ISA are addressed in the four ELT workbooks. In this workbook on sharing faith you will work on the following sixteen skills measured by the ISA, skills associated with sharing faith, leading teams, and building relationships with unchurched people:

- I have recruited and equipped a team of five or more people to conduct an evangelistic event or service.

- I have started a ministry team from scratch.

- I have started a Bible study or small group from scratch.

- I have started a Bible study or small group that included seekers.

- I have started a Bible study or small group that included seekers which grew to more than 10 people.

- I have been part of a team that started a Bible study or small group or other ministry.

- I have shared my faith with _____ people in the last year.

- I have led _____ adults (over 18 years old) to salvation.

- I have led _____ adults to salvation that I did not first meet through church.

- I have led _____ adults (over 18 years old) to salvation in the last year.

- I have led _____ teens (ages 13-18) to salvation in the last year.

- I have trained _____ people in evangelism.

- I have planned and done something socially with _____ number of non-Christian(s) who were not family members in the past year.

- I have served _____ number of non-Christian(s) who were not family members in the past year.

- I have invited _____ unchurched person to come to church with me this year.

- I have invited _____ unchurched people to come to church with me this year, and they came.

When you complete the two-year ELT you will have raised your skill level as a missional Christian leader and your scores on the ISA.

Working with an ELT Module

Each module includes the following elements to facilitate adult learning:

- **Reading:** Core reading provides essential content for each module.

- **Workbook:** The heart of the module is this workbook. The workbook presents important insights and guided exercises that will develop your missional leadership skills. The workbook is yours to keep.

- **Personal Answer Book:** Your personal answer book includes the core exercises you will complete as you go through the module workbook. Download it at http://kairoschurchplanting.org/resources/emerging-leader-training/

- **Webinar:** Periodically, experienced church plant leaders will lead webinars from their own missional experiences and experiments—what worked, what didn't and what they've learned along the way. You can access these webinars at kairoschurchplanting.org

- **Missional Director:** In your church context you will work under the guidance of a missional director, typically a church staff minister, who will monitor your progress, help you process your reading and experiences, and direct you as you practice missional leadership.

- **Strategy Assignment:** Each module culminates in a strategy assignment that applies your learning in an integrated activity. The strategy assignement is the most important exercise in the module.

Completing an ELT Module

To complete an ELT module you must successfully accomplish the following:

- Complete the workbook and reading assignments.

- Receive positive evaluations from your missional director.

- Accomplish your strategy assignment.

- Email or mail your completed personal answer book to us at KairosTraining@kairoschurchplanting.org or 11124 NE Halsey St. #497, Portland, OR 97220. When you complete year one you will receive a Certificate of Basic Church Leadership and a Certificate of Advanced Church Leadership when you complete the modules for year two.

Sharing Faith

Lesson 1: About this Module

In this module you will practice one of the great spiritual disciplines: Sharing Faith. This is not a discipline you will read about in Richard Foster's *Celebration of Discipline*.[1] It is not found among the sixty disciplines included in Adele Ahlburg Calhoun's *Spiritual Disciplines Handbook*.[2] It is, however, one of the essential disciplines of following Jesus. In this module, we will spend time in the gospel accounts of the Great Commission in which Jesus told his disciples to share their faith in him.

This module consists of four essential components:

1. Readings

- Bill Hybels and Mark Mittelberg. *Becoming a Contagious Christian*. Zondervan, 1996.

- Garry Poole. *Seeker Small Groups*. Zondervan, 2003.

2. Workbook

The workbook is your primary guide. It is designed with questions and exercises for you to complete. You will keep the workbook as your record of your spiritual journey into leadership.

3. Answer Book

Download a copy of your personal answer book at http://kairoschurchplanting.org/resources/emerging-leader-training/ and use it to re-complete the exercises in this workbook. On completing this module, send your personal answer book and strategy assignment materials to

Kairos Church Planting
11124 NE Halsey St. #497
Portland, OR 97220

or email them to KairosTraining@kairoschurchplanting.org.

---

1. HarperCollins, 3rd ed., 1988.
2. InterVarsity, 2006.

4. The Great Commissions

When someone says "the Great Commission," your mind probably goes to Matthew 20:18-20, the passage known historically by that name. In fact, scripture gives us the final, great commission of Jesus in five different forms, one in each of the four gospels and one in the Acts of the Apostles.

William L. Banks, in his book *In Search of the Great Commission*, says this about these different gospel perspectives on the Great Commission:

Each gospel has its own thrust and emphasis. Each presents Christ in a different manner, and the presentation of the Great Commission in each gospel is varied. The reader is led to consider the Great Commission from a different perspective in each gospel, beginning with the very day on which Christ arose from the dead.[3]

We will use the four gospel commissioning records as starting points for theological reflection on a range of biblical teachings important to our sharing faith. I've chosen to pursue these commissioning statements in chronological order of their time of writing. We'll begin with Mark 16:15-16, the earliest written record, then move to Matthew 28:18-20, Luke 24:46-49, and end with John 20:21, the last gospel to be written.

5. Strategy Assignment

The strategy assignment is a summative activity that incorporates your studies from this module into an integrated activity. For this module you will lead a small evangelism team of faith sharers to gather faith seekers together for a five-week seeker group experience using the Sycamore Series *Life* book.

This workbook is meant to be completed across six months. Don't think of it as merely a set of course requirements, but as a tool to help you develop. Development takes time, energy, and reflection. You can't make yourself grow, but you can give yourself the opportunity to grow.

---

3. William L. Banks. *In Search of the Great Commission: What Did Jesus Really Say?* (Chicago: Moody, 1991), 13.

Module Objectives: Action Steps

The *Sharing Faith* module is intended to help you develop your motivation for and skill at sharing your faith as a lifelong spiritual discipline. As you do this you will not only develop your own practice and ways of sharing faith, you will lead others to do so as well. The following is a list of action steps you will take throughout this module.

Unit A—Starting Points
- ❑ 60-Second Faith Statement
- ❑ Kairos Evangelism Assessment
- ❑ Prayer Team Celebration
- ❑ Email Your Prayer Team
- ❑ Restaurant Praying

Unit B—Understanding Unbelief
- ❑ 3 Question Conversations
- ❑ Prayer Focus List
- ❑ Spiritual Diagnosis

Unit C—Conversion
- ❑ Write Your Personal Conversion Story
- ❑ Your Spritual Journey Guide

Unit D—Connecting with God's Lost People
- ❑ Conversation—What Do People Think About God?
- ❑ Order the Sycamore Training Materials for Your Seeker Group
- ❑ Assemble Your Team

Unit E—Creating Seeker Groups
- ❑ Invite Seekers
- ❑ Recruit Host and Childcare Helpers
- ❑ Funnel of Consideration

Unit F—Strategy Assignment
- ❑ Team Training
- ❑ Seeker Meetings
- ❑ Follow-up Calls
- ❑ Follow-up Meetings

Missional Director Meetings

The Paul/Timothy model is a powerful example of the relationship between an experienced leader and an emerging leader. This model is more than just a mentoring relationship. It is a training relationship. Paul took Timothy with him as he engaged in his own ministry. As Timothy grew in experience, Paul assigned leadership tasks for Timothy to practice his own leadership abilities. Ultimately, Timothy, a mature leader in his own right, assumed the lead ministry role at Ephesus (I Timothy).

We believe that having a training relationship in a church context will multiply your growth process. If you have yet to do so, identify a missional director in your church, preferably a staff minister. It could also be an elder or, in some cases, a leader in a specific ministry in your church. Your missional director should meet the following criteria:

- Be currently employed by your church, have a background as a church minister, or be recognized as a spiritual leader in your church.

- Be someone you respect and wish to learn from.

- Have the time and interest to do the following:

    - Monitor your progress.

    - Meet with you five times in the next six months for two hours each meeting.

    - Prepare for these meetings by reading the two assigned books and following along in the workbook as you work through the assignments.

    - Be available to talk over questions when you have them, recommend other resources to you, and open doors for other experiences he or she thinks will help you grow as a godly leader.

During your first meeting with your missional director, which you should have before the end of the first lesson, do the following:

- Pray together.

- Read the ELT Relationship Covenant in your personal answer book aloud together and sign it. If you are working towards a certificate of completion, photocopy the covenant page and send it to Kairos at 11124 NE Halsey St., #497, Portland, OR 97220. Or, scan and e-mail it to KairosTraining@kairoschurchplanting.org.

- Set the date for your second meeting.

- Talk about your expectations and hopes for your development as a missional leader through the ELT and this module on sharing faith. Discuss the following questions:

What are you excited about in this module on sharing faith?

_____

_____

_____

What challenges do you anticipate?

_____

_____

_____

What goals do you have in mind for yourself?

_____

_____

_____

How do you anticipate this module impacting your leadership in your church?

_____

_____

_____

What outcomes do you anticipate?

_____

_____

_____

Look over your anticipated timeline for completing this module on page vii. Talk through the timing, potential interferences, and why you are committing to this learning experience.

Unit A
Starting Points

Clive Staples Lewis[4] was arguably the most influential atheist turned Christian apologist of the twentieth century.

Lewis's journey into unbelief began as a child when he and his brother Warren were made to sit and listen to the unimaginative sermons of their maternal Grandfather Hamilton, rector of Saint Mark's in Dundela, Ireland. Reflecting on these moments, Lewis recounts he was offered only "the dry husk of Christianity." As a young adult, he returned from military service on the Western Front during World War I "wounded, lonely and more introspective than before."[5]

Consider these words from Lewis's autobiography, *Surprised by Joy* (1955).

You must picture me alone in that room in Magdalen, night after night, feeling, whenever my mind lifted even for a second from my work, the steady, unrelenting approach of Him whom I so earnestly desired not to meet. That which I greatly feared had at last come upon me. In the Trinity Term of 1929 I gave in, and admitted that God was God, and knelt and prayed: perhaps, that night, the most dejected and reluctant convert in all England.[6]

C.S. Lewis

What Lewis experienced—his fears of becoming a Christian, the pursuing God of joy, and the influences of fellow faith travelers—are common elements to the stories of people moving from unbelief to belief. In *Sharing Faith* we will further explore this process of conversion.

There are two important points I want you to understand as we begin *Sharing Faith*. First, you are a critical person of influence on people around you. These people's faith lives—and fears—are similar to Lewis's. Second, your role in their faith story is always secondary to God's role. God pursues people in order to lavish upon them all the love and compassion he displayed through the incarnation of Jesus.

---

4. Photo source: http://classicalworld.files.wordpress.com/2010/02/cs-lewis2.jpg?w=150&h=148

5. George Sayer, *Jack: A Life of C.S. Lewis* (Wheaton, IL: Crossway, 2005), 217-218.

6. C.S. Lewis, *Surprised by Joy: The Shape of My Early Life*, revised ed. (Orlando, FL: Houghton Mifflin Harcourt, 1995).

Lesson 2: Assessing Your Evangelism

Kairos Church Planting works extensively with men and women in whom God has placed the vision for a new church. We work with these men and women through assessment, training, and coaching to encourage and support them in their church planting ministries. One of the assessment tools we use is the Initial Screening Assessment. In the *Spiritual Formation* module you were asked to take the Initial Screening Assessment (ISA) at churchplanterprofiles.com. If you have not taken that assessment, I encourage you to do so now. It is free when you sign up for an account. When you create your account, scroll to the end of the page and select Kairos Church Planting as your agency.

It may or may not surprise you that among the four areas measured by the ISA—1) Church Planting, 2) Entrepreneurial Leadership, 3) Ministry Experience, and 4) Relational Evangelism—Relational Evangelism has the lowest median score at 48%. This overall score reflects our experience at Kairos. It seems few people, even ministers, have developed the spiritual discipline of sharing faith.

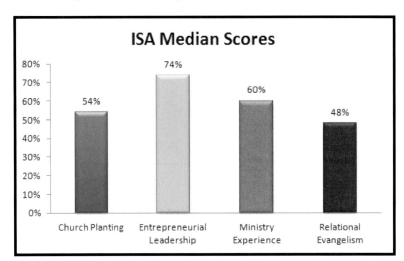

My friend and one time coach, Gary Rohrmayer[7], in his book *Spiritual Conversations,* surmises that most Christians have matured beyond their level of obedience. By this, he means that though we have advanced in age, we still act like teenagers in our faith. Perhaps he is right. We don't fail to share our faith because we lack knowledge, but because we don't practice sharing it.

As a quick start, take this one question evangelism survey. With which statement do you find yourself agreeing most?

- ❏ I love to share my faith.
- ❏ I am terrified to share my faith.
- ❏ I never share my faith.
- ❏ I don't know how to share my faith.

---

7. Gary served as the national director of Converge USA's church planting ministry from 2006-2010, which Ed Stetzer calls the most effective mid-size church planting ministry in America.

We'll dig deeper into your evangelism experience later. For now, just keep this quick peek in mind.

The Great Commission

Mark 16:15-16—Gospel Content

He said to them, "Go into all the world and preach the gospel to all creation. Whoever believes and is baptized will be saved, but whoever does not believe will be condemned."

In Mark's unique, "straight on" approach, his record of Jesus's commission is succinct and to the point. The operative verb in Mark's version of the Great Commission is "preach." It is unfortunate that in English we cannot gather the force of Mark's words. In our translations the command appears to be GO because that is what comes first. In what Mark wrote, however, his command is PREACH the gospel. PREACH is the imperative. Salvation or condemnation lies in the balance.

Mark's command is to preach the gospel. So, what is this gospel we are to proclaim?

The Content of Gospel

Mark brackets his book with what was in his day a new literary term—gospel. The Greek word for gospel, *euanggelion,* means good news. Mark begins his writing with the words, "This is the Good News (gospel) about Jesus the Messiah, the Son of God (Mark 1:1)." He ends his book with the Great Commission and the command to preach the gospel. In between these gospel bookends Mark provides the content of this gospel. The gospel is good news and the good news is Jesus, what he said and did as he fulfilled his purpose as the visible incarnation of God. As the Hebrew writer said in Hebrews 1:3, *"The Son radiates God's own glory and expresses the very character of God."*

Christ's incarnation was more than just being God on earth. Immanuel (God with us, Matthew 1:23) came to save sinners (Luke 16:10). The theological shorthand for this purpose of Jesus' time on earth is called substitutionary atonement. Substitutionary atonement refers to Jesus' death on the cross as a substitute for sinners, as a payment for the consequences of sin. The biblical storyline, beginning with Genesis, is that the world God created was perfect but that human overreaching and rebellion broke the relationship between God and people. The rest of scripture describes God's pursuit of his lost people to redeem them back to himself through a perfect sacrifice—Jesus.

The theme of substitutionary atonement runs throughout the Bible. Below is a list of scriptures that simplifies the essence of Jesus' atonement.

- **Romans 3:12; 23**—*All have turned away; all have become useless. No one does good, not a single one. For everyone has sinned; we all fall short of God's glorious standard.*

- **Romans 6:23**—*For the wages of sin is death, but the free gift of God is eternal life through Christ Jesus our Lord.*

- **2 Corinthians 5:21**—*He made Him who knew no sin to be sin on our behalf, that we might become the righteousness of God in Him.*

- **Romans 4:25**—*He was delivered up because of our transgressions, and was raised because of our justification.*

- **Isaiah 53:4-5**—*Surely our griefs He Himself bore, and our sorrows He carried; yet we ourselves esteemed Him stricken, smitten of God, and afflicted. But He was pierced through for our transgressions. He was crushed for our iniquities. The chastening for our well-being fell upon Him and by His scourging we are healed.*

Jesus' death as Immanuel is the climaxing event of God's pursuing love. It was the sacrifice of the Lamb of God on our behalf (Revelation 5:1-6; 7:14). This was Jesus' substituionary atonement.

Action Step

Put together your best 60-second presentation of the gospel.

When I was on the faculty of Cascade College in Portland, OR, I was blessed to teach a capstone Bible class called Senior Bible Seminar. We used a great book on Christian apologetics by Lee Strobel, *The Case for Faith.*[8] Strobel was an atheistic journalist who set out to prove Christianity was not true and ended up a Christ follower instead. In class we would talk through each chapter then some students would give what we called our "60 second faith statement." In 60 seconds they were to give their best answer to that objection to Christianity.

One week we were talking over the objection, "It's offensive to claim Jesus is the only way to God." Two male students and I went out on our Max Train (Portland city's light rail) to talk to people about Jesus. It happened the two men they chose to talk with were gay. When my students introduced themselves and made their opening statement these two men did what I call the "spiritual vomit." They spewed out what they thought would be the most offensive thing they could say to Christians, "We don't believe in Jesus, we're gay."

"WE DON'T BELIEVE IN JESUS— WE'RE GAY."

I watched my two guys struggle through that blast, then one of them did something most insightful. He reached his hand out and laid it on the shoulder of the speaker and said, "That's all right. We just want to listen to what you have to say." That touch and the willingness to listen opened up a twenty-minute conversation that continued until we had to get off to return to the college. I believe my students gave a great answer about faith in Jesus to those two men. It didn't even take sixty seconds, just a warm touch and an open conversation.

---

8. *The Case for Faith: A Journalist Investigates the Toughest Objections to Christianity* (Grand Rapids, MI: Zondervan, 2000).

If someone said to you, "Why are you a Christian?" how would you answer? Make notes. Practice what you would say. Time yourself.

Here's the scary part. After you've practiced, share your 60-second gospel presentation with a friend who is not yet a believer. An easy way to do this is to tell your friend you are taking a course and this is one of your assignments. Ask your friend to help you by timing you and listening to you. Ask for feedback. Did it make sense? Were you able to say it well? How close were you to sixty seconds?

Reporting

Turn to lesson 2 in your Personal Answer Book and record this assignment.

Reading: Hybels, chapters 1-2

Becoming a Contagious Christian is not a recent book, but it is still a powerful and accessible introduction to sharing faith. Whether you are a fan of Bill Hybels or not, you are probably aware of the Willow Creek Church in the South Barrington suburb of Chicago. Hybels and his plant team began what became known as the "seeker sensitive" style of church on October 12, 1975, with one hundred and twenty-five people at their first worship service. Today, through speaking, writing, and the Willow Creek Association, Bill Hybels is one of the most well-known Christian leaders in the world. Willow Creek Community Church was the third largest church in America in 2012 with over 24,200 attending services each weekend.[9]

What you may not know about Bill is that early in his life he gave up the rights to a family industrial fortune by choosing to go into ministry rather than pursuing a career in his family business. Bill's father literally wrote Bill out of his will, not to punish his son for pursuing ministry, but to take away a potential life preserver. In a real way, Bill understood that ministry was to be an "all or nothing" proposition.

As you read *Contagious Christian*, I am going to guide your interaction with the book through a series of attention exercises. These exercises are designed to draw your attention to ideas and how they impact you as you develop your practice of sharing faith.

Chapter One

Hybels wants us to investigate our motives for sharing faith by asking us to answer this question: *why does sharing faith matter to God?* Hybels finds his answer to this question in Luke 15 in the parables of the lost sheep, coin, and sons.

What about you? If you were to settle on one biblical passage, story,

---

9. "100 Largest Churches in America," in *Outreach Special Issue* (2012): 35.

or theme that answers the question, "Why does sharing faith matter to God?" what would it be? Explain why you chose this passage.

Biblical passage:

_____

Why did you choose this one?

_____

_____

_____

Hybels also tells us the stories of two people with whom he deliberately cultivated personal relationships. Read these two stories again and identify as many characteristics or insights about these two men as

Tom	Muslim Indian
_____	_____
_____	_____
_____	_____
_____	_____
_____	_____
_____	_____
_____	_____
_____	_____
_____	_____

you can. Record your observations on the lines provided.

Chapter Two

"Cost/benefit ratios" is not a typical term we use in a church context, yet Hybels asks us to consider it.

Think about your involvement as a faith-sharing disciple. If you make sharing faith a consistent spiritual discipline in your life, what are the benefits you can anticipate accruing? What costs can you anticipate?

AND WHILE HE WAS STILL A LONG WAY OFF, HIS FATHER SAW HIM COMING. FILLED WITH LOVE AND COMPASSION, HE RAN TO HIS SON, EMBRACED HIM, AND KISSED HIM.

LUKE 15:21

Benefits	Costs
_____	_____
_____	_____
_____	_____
_____	_____
_____	_____
_____	_____
_____	_____
_____	_____
_____	_____

Evangelism Assessment

I carefully chose the idea of "sharing faith" instead of a title including the word "evangelism" for this workbook. You see, evangelism has become something of an unclean, emotionally charged word. Evangelism is one of those guilt-producing words that makes us think, "I know I should do it, but I don't want to." One of our planters made a comment about his emotional reaction to evangelism. His sentiment may resonate with you. He said, "Coming from the heritage we come from, evangelism is sold to believers as a really cut and dry thing, right? Tell them the truth, plot the path to salvation, and boom, dunk them! . . . That story didn't connect, convict, or persuade anyone that God was anything more that a bully, or, for our atheist friends, a weak system of leveraging guilt onto people so that one would feel compelled to a set of rules/morality."

How does the word *evangelism* make you feel?

_____
_____
_____
_____

A bit further into this workbook, we'll look at Tim Keller's idea of cultural defeater beliefs. But right now we've got to at least recognize our own Christian defeater beliefs. These Christian defeater beliefs are what cause us to shrink away from the act of, and even the word, evangelism. These defeater beliefs are what keep our mouths shut and locked, or cause our tongues to stammer when we even think about saying the name of Jesus to people around us.

I observe the following three active Christian defeater beliefs:

1. We're kind of embarrassed to talk about Jesus. We know that Jesus, church, religion, etc. are not really acceptable topics of conversation. In fact, these are more conversation stoppers than starters.

2. We know there's a reputation out there that Christians can be petty, mean, cruel, and homophobic. We probably each have some story of a Christian who acted boorishly. We don't want to be "guilty by association."

3. We fear people will reject us. They'll put is in the camp of "undesirable" people and ostracize us from their social networks.

Embarrassment   Reputation   Fear

These words represent our Christian defeater beliefs, those emotionally active responses that we often associate with the word evangelism. "Evangelism" carries its own history and baggage. In this book, we'll talk about sharing faith.

Before we move on, let's dwell on Hebrews 13:15.

Through Jesus, therefore, let us continually offer to God a sacrifice of praise—the fruit of lips that confess his name.

Sharing faith is confession. It is one of our ways to praise God. If we don't learn the practice of sharing our faith, we run the risk of both denying Jesus and losing an avenue of praise to God.

In the *Spiritual Formation* module, I referred to spiritual disciplines as those ways in which we practice our relationship with God. I defined a spiritual discipline as "an intentional, planned practice of relation that leads to spiritual maturity in specific and measurable ways (p. 70)." In this module we're shifting our focus from the inward journey of spiritual discipline to the outward discipline of sharing faith.

What do you think of the idea that sharing faith is an essential spiritual discipline for a mature Christ follower?

_____

_____

_____

_____

_____

_____

How does viewing sharing faith as an essential spiritual discipline make you feel?

_____

_____

_____

_____

_____

_____

If the idea that sharing faith is an essential spiritual discipline for a Christ follower intimidates you, you are not alone. Many Christ followers in our churches have been Christians for years but have not matured as faith-sharing disciples. It's no wonder that for the last thirty or more years most evangelical congregations average only one conversion baptism for every eighty plus members[10] or that in the average year fifty percent of churches will not add one new member through conversion![11] If a majority of Christians matured in this area of discipleship, truly the world would feel the presence of God's people.

Now let's get to that point you may have been dreading—or maybe the one you've been eager to get to.

How you are doing as a disciple who shares faith?

Giftedness for Sharing Faith

Your giftedness set is composed of natural talents, acquired skills, and spiritually endowed gifts. If you completed the first Emerging Leadership Training module, *Spiritual Formation*, you diagrammed your giftedness set on page 65. Go back to that set and copy your gifts here. If you have not done the *Spiritual Formation* module, use the following descriptions to do a quick listing of your gifts.

10. Flavil Yeakley, *Why Churches Grow* (Wichita, KS: Christian Communications, 1979), 6, and Thom Rainer, *Surprising Insights from the Unchurched and Proven Ways to Reach Them* (Wheaton, IL: Zondervan, 2001), 23.

11. Ron Sylvia, *High Definition Church Planting* (Ocala, FL: High Definition Resources, 2006), 26.

Natural Talents (capacities or abilities you were born with) *example: outgoing personality*	Acquired Skills (talents and capabilities you have acquired through practice and application) *example: speed reading*	Spiritual Gifts (God-given capacities received from the Holy Spirit) *example: spiritual discernment*

CIRCLE the items you listed that you think are important or useful for sharing faith with others.

Look at the items you circled. How well prepared or capable do you think you are to be a disciple who shares faith as a spiritual discipline?

Action Step

Go to the Kairos website (kairoschurchplanting.org). Under the planter tab, click on *Steps to Becoming a Church Planter* and then the *Evangelism Assessment* button to download the Kairos Evangelism Assessment. Take the assessment before answering the following questions.

In which of the four areas did you score the highest?

_____

In which did you score the lowest?

_____

What have you learned about yourself and sharing faith from your Evangelism Assessment?

_____

_____

_____

_____

_____

_____

_____

_____

Reporting

Go to your Personal Answer Book and record your scores for the Evangelism Assessment.

Your Personal Prayer Team

One of the activities in the *Spiritual Formation* module was to organize and lead an intimate prayer team on your behalf as you began the process of deliberately developing yourself as a godly leader. If you have not already done so, encourage your prayer team with a celebration event. It doesn't have to be anything major, but do something that expresses your gratitude to the people who have been praying for you. Take this opportunity to share with them that you are now learning about and practicing sharing faith.

If you did not complete the *Spiritual Formation* module, an intimate prayer team is a small group of people you invite to pray for you weekly. The following section will walk you through how to form your prayer team.

Action Step

If you do not have a personal prayer team to pray with you and for you as you work through this Emerging Leader Training series, form one now. Invite three or four people to be on your prayer team. Here's what they will do:

1. Pray for you weekly. You may think that they will do this easily. Probably not. Many have lost the habit of consistent, intercessory prayer. As a leader your role is to influence them back into this habit. Do this by:

- Weekly personal prayer time with at least one person on your prayer team either in person or over the phone. If people have not prayed over the phone before they may feel uncomfortable with this practice at first. Encourage one another in this distance prayer and you may find it very enjoyable.

- Send weekly email or text message updates to everyone that they can use to pray for you specifically.

- Periodically call your prayer team to meet together for group prayer. Also, people really enjoy celebrations, so if God answers a prayer in an obvious way call your team together to celebrate! Eat ice cream. Throw a party. Do something significant to celebrate God's activity.

2. Pray for your church's passion for God's lost people in your community. Raise the consciousness of your prayer team to pray for your church.

3. Be part of a prayer network. Kairos is developing a national prayer network for God's lost people in America. Our goal is for one thousand people to give ten minutes a month of dedicated prayer for God's lost sons and daughters. You and your prayer team can join this movement at kairosprayer.org.

Reporting

Complete the prayer team page in your personal answer book.

Lesson 3: Seeing God's Lost People

The 1999 Bruce Willis movie thriller *The Sixth Sense*[12] is about a boy who communicates with spirits who don't know they're dead. This was one of those movies where I thought I knew what was going to happen and thought I was prepared for it—but, nope. They got me anyway. The punch line of the movie is, "I see dead people."

Do you see dead people? I don't mean the ghostly characters of *The Sixth Sense*. I mean the real flesh and blood people who are all around you but who don't have true life. Seeing dead people is a skill you need to develop.

Universalism

Universalism is the belief that God will eventually save everyone. It is the idea that ultimately God's love wins, that heaven is everything, and that hell is just a bad story designed to scare people. The problem with universalism is that it doesn't square with biblical teaching.

Blueletterbible.org is a wonderful Bible search tool. Go to the website now. On the top right hand side you'll see a "Search the Bible" box. Type "judgment" in the search box, select a Bible version—say NLT (New Living Translation). Click on the *Range Options* and type in Mat-Rev for Matthew-Revelation.

How many times does "judgment" occur in the New Testament in the NLT?

_____

Read through some of these judgment texts. At the bottom of your results page click on 2. (John 12:48-2, Pet. 2:4). Scroll down to 1 Peter 4:17. Read 1 Peter 4:12-19 and consider it in the larger biblical context.

How do these judgment texts relate to the universalist idea that everyone will ultimately be saved?

_____

_____

_____

_____

_____

_____

_____

12. Photo source: http://tvtropes.org/pmwiki/pmwiki.php/Film/TheSixthSense?from=Main.TheSixthSense

The relevance of being critically aware of universalism and its emotional pull is illustrated by the controversy over the book *Love Wins* (HarperOne, 2011) by Rob Bell. Bell has a large influence among many Christians. In *Love Wins* Bell argues a traditional universalist message, that ultimately God's love will triumph over all human sin and rebellion and everyone will be saved.

The idea that God could not and would not judge anybody is a powerfully attractive idea, but it is not a biblically acceptable belief. Two books I recommend on the subject are edited by Christopher W. Morgan and Robert A. Peterson: *Faith Comes by Hearing: A Response to Inclusivism* (IVP Academic, 2008) and *Hell Under Fire: Modern Scholarship Reinvents Eternal Punishment* (Zondervan, 2004). These books cover a wide range of topics including views on heaven and hell, God's justice, and the nature of salvation.

Here are four points to consider about universalism:

1. Universalism undercuts the nature of God as a just and righteous God by pitting his loving nature against his righteousness.

2. Universalism requires an alternative method of salvation that bypasses belief and confession of Jesus Christ as Lord.[13]

3. Universalism denies the existence of an eternal hell.

4. Universalism nullifies the atoning death of Jesus.

Reading: Hybels, chapters 3-4

Hybels starts us off by calling attention to the "ought to" dilemma. We know what we ought to do but not how to do it. This "ought to" dilemma is particularly strong in the context of sharing faith. We know we ought to be faith sharers, but it feels so intimidating, so inauthentic, so politically incorrect.

Share this dilemma in your own words.

Sharing faith is hard for me because

_____

_____

_____

_____

_____

_____

Hybels presents us with a challenge. How can we have maximum spiritual influence on the people around us? I hope this question raises a new level of expectation, that it spurs you to consider different approaches to communicating gospel to different audiences. In a later

13. Banks, *Great Commission*, 63.

module called *Essential Leadership*, I'll address the idea of preaching in the context of belief and unbelief. For now I'll summarize the essential difference between these two approaches. Preaching to belief is focused on confirming what is already known so the audience leaves affirmed. Preaching to unbelief addresses the unsettled questions of life. It changes the type of engagement we expect of preaching.

Hybels changes our level of engagement in the expectations we have of ourselves as disciples. It is not good enough to be good. Disciples must be productive or, in Hybel's word, impacting.

Here is the maximum impact formula Hybels sees for discipleship:

High Potency + Close Proximity + Clear Communication = Maximum Impact

Provide your understanding for each component of Hybel's formula.

High Potency

_____

_____

Close Proximity

_____

_____

Clear Communication

_____

_____

Maximum Impact

_____

_____

Action Step

Prepare an email for your prayer team with a specific request about who you want to become as a disciple who has maximum spiritual impact on the people around you. Compose your email here and then send it off to them.

_____

_____

_____

_____

_____

_____

_____

_____

_____

_____

Cultural Unbelief

We live in a culture where unbelief has become the norm. In their book *unChristian*, David Kinnamon and Gabe Lyons[14] present research on how the Buster (born between 1965 and 1980) and Mosaic (born between 1980 and 2002) generations view and feel about Christianity. Here are some of their findings:

- Fewer than one out of ten young adults mention faith as their top priority, despite the fact that the vast majority of Busters and Mosaics attended a Christian church during their high school years (p. 23).

- Nearly two out of every five young outsiders (38 percent) claim to have a "bad impression of present-day Christianity" (p. 24).

- One third of young outsiders said that Christianity represents a negative image with which they would not want to be associated. This group is at least three times larger than it was in 1992 (p. 24).

- The three most common perceptions of present-day Christianity are that it is:

  ➡ Antihomosexual (an image held by 91 percent of young outsiders)

  ➡ Judgmental (87 percent)

  ➡ Hypocritical (85 percent)

- Out of the top 12 perceptions of Christianity, nine views were negative (p. 27).

These findings probably do not surprise you. If you are a Buster or a Mosiac, this is your world. Is it any wonder then that we struggle to be disciples who share our faith regularly and freely when Christianity and biblical faith are so negatively perceived by the people around us?

It's tempting to think how easy it was for the first Christians to share their faith. After all, they had Jesus, Peter, Paul and the other apostles right there with them. Turn to 1 Peter 4:12-19 and read Peter's encouragement to those Christians living in Galatia, today's Turkey. From this description, I don't think it was easy for them to share their faith. In fact, the reason Peter wrote this letter to these Christians is because

14. David Kinnamon and Gabe Lyons, *unChristian: What a New Generation Really Thinks about Christianity...and Why It Matters* (Grand Rapids, MI: Baker, 2007).

they were struggling.

Look at what Peter tells these Christ followers:

- Don't be surprised at the fiery trials you are going through.

- Be glad for the trials because you are partners in suffering with Christ.

- Be happy when you are insulted for being a Christian.

- It is no shame to suffer for being a Christian.

These statements certainly don't sound like the Galatian Christians were having an easy time of it. They lived among people who mistrusted them and who thought they were bad people. Roman senator and historian Tacitus wrote about the persecution of Christians in *The Annals*. The following excerpt, written around 116 A.D., tells about the burning of Rome during the time of the emperor Nero.

> *Consequently, to get rid of the report, Nero fastened the guilt and inflicted the most exquisite tortures on a class hated for their abominations, called Christians by the populace. Christus, from whom the name had its origin, suffered the extreme penalty during the reign of Tiberius at the hands of one of our procurators, Pontius Pilatus, and a most mischievous superstition, thus checked for the moment, again broke out not only in Judæa, the first source of the evil, but even in Rome, where all things hideous and shameful from every part of the world find their centre and become popular. Accordingly, an arrest was first made of all who pleaded guilty; then, upon their information, an immense multitude was convicted, not so much of the crime of firing the city, as of hatred against mankind.*[15]

I imagine these early Christians were afraid to share their faith, and no wonder. I suspect the most powerful factor that keeps you from sharing your faith is also fear. We fear rejection. We fear how people will view us as believers. We fear that we will lose the respect or friendship of those with whom we wish to be associated.

The only way to get over—or perhaps beyond—such fear is to practice sharing faith.

Action Step

This week begin the weekly practice of praying for people who serve you at restaurants. Go to a restaurant where there is staff that serves your table. When your server comes to take your order say,

"We're (I'm) going to share a prayer in a few minutes, is there anything we (I) can bless you with through prayer?"

---

15. Tacitus, *Annals*, book 15, chapter 44.

Felicia

I pray for wait staff regularly. Most of the time the waiters or waitresses have a positive response.

A while ago I was with a group of three other men, all ministers, in Austin, Texas. We went to eat lunch at a very popular, busy restaurant. As I looked around at the wait staff I saw sleeve tattoos, piercings in various parts of ears, noses, and eyebrows, a variety of color dyed hair. I felt like I was home in Portland! Our waitress had purple hair and a full sleeve tat on one arm. A tattoo of the top of a sailing ship's masts could be seen at the neckline of her shirt.

When she took our order I said, "We're going to share a prayer in a few minutes, is there anything we can bless you with through prayer?" She politely deflected my question. I made a comment about her tat sleeve and told her she had to tell us about her tattoos. She left to put our order in. When she got back her first words were, "And the tat across my chest . . ." and she went on to explain what the ship meant to her.

Her name was Felicia. She gave us the "spiritual vomit." Felicia was throwing something at us to put us off. Unbelievers want to see how we'll react. Will we emotionally jump back, or will we accept what they say and continue to engage with them?

We learned more about Felicia during the course of our lunch—how old she was, how long she'd been a waitress, the fact that she wanted to visit Portland some day.

It can be hard to gauge what happens inside a person during one of these conversations. I bet when Felicia awoke that morning the last thing she would have anticipated was an encounter with God. Yet when we take an extra step or two into someone's life and offer an encounter with faith, God steps in in a visible, personal way. It's our calling as Christians to allow God pathways into the lives of people around us. Felicia enjoyed that encounter. I know from the note she left on our receipt.

Reporting

When you have prayed for a wait staff write about your experience under Lesson 3 in your Personal Answer Book.

Unit B
Understanding Unbelief

Antony Garrard Newton Flew (1923-2010)[1] was the most influential atheist of the second half of the twentieth century. Flew was a British philosopher, educated at Oxford. While a student at Oxford, Flew often attended the weekly meetings of C.S. Lewis's Socratic Club. Despite the influence of Lewis, whom Flew regarded as the most powerful Christian apologist of his day, Flew rejected Lewis's moral argument for God as well as the classic ontological and teleological arguments for God. In 1950 Flew presented a paper at the Socratic Club titled "Theology and Falsification" in which he argued that the statements of religious belief were meaningless and that the assertion that God exists has no argument to prove it. In 1961 Flew published *God and Philosophy*, which placed him as the recognized champion of the atheistic position. Other writings followed including *The Presumption of Atheism* (1971) *and Atheistic Humanism* (1993).

Flew shocked the philosophical world at a panel of religious scholars at New York University in 2004 when he revealed that he had changed his mind and now accepted the existence of God. Flew related in his final book, *There is a God: How the World's Most Notorious Atheist Changed His Mind* (2007), how it was the weight of biological research that ultimately changed his mind. In his April 13, 2010 obituary, *The Telegraph* reported Flew's decision.

Antony Garrard Newton Flew

After months of soul-searching, Flew concluded that research into DNA had "shown, by the almost unbelievable complexity of the arrangements which are needed to produce life, that intelligence must have been involved." Moreover, though he accepted Darwinian evolution, he felt that it could not explain the beginnings of life. "I have been persuaded that it is simply out of the question that the first living matter evolved out of dead matter and then developed into an extraordinarily complicated creature," he said.

Unbelief is a culture, a context. In fact, unbelief is a worldview, a set of assumptions about what is true and what is not true, what exists and what doesn't exist, and how one is supposed to act because of those beliefs. We Christians have a worldview that is both cultural and faith-based. This Christian worldview is premised on our belief in God as the good creator and Jesus as the redeeming Lord. People who do not believe in God also have a worldview that is both cultural and faith-based. They believe that a good creator God doesn't exist and that there is no redeeming Lord Jesus. In this unit we will investigate who God's lost people are and why they don't believe.

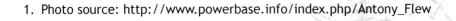

1. Photo source: http://www.powerbase.info/index.php/Antony_Flew

Lesson 4: Who Are God's Lost People?

This story from Jason Whaley, a missionary in Wollongong, Australia, illustrates a faith encounter that touched the worldview core of unbelief.

David is an IT graduate student from China living in Wollongong. One day David heard Corey talk on "The Kingdom of God" during our event at the community centre. Afterward David told us, "I don't believe in God, but that's an awesome message!"

One night I (Jason) thought David could help me understand Jesus better. I asked him if he could explain to me what an algorithm is since math is his second language. He did and I asked a few more questions. Finally I said, "That's something I believe about Jesus, that he's the algorithm of the universe." The look that came over David's face was as though he understood what I had said even more than I did.

Later David opened up to me, "To be honest with you, I'm checking you guys out to see if this is something I want for my life. I never believed in God before, but what you're describing and the way you're living makes more sense of my past experiences in my life than anything else."

Sometimes before people can come to belief, they first have to understand their own unbelief. David took it for granted that God didn't exist, but once he saw his own unbelief, the idea of belief in God made more sense.

The Great Commission

Mark 16:15-16—The Exclusive Gospel

He said to them, "Go into all the world and preach the gospel to all creation. Whoever believes and is baptized will be saved, but whoever does not believe will be condemned.

The second half of Mark's presentation of the Great Commission (v.16) raises questions about the gospel's exclusive claims and the consequences of belief in the gospel for salvation or condemnation. Our culture struggles against the idea that Jesus offers the only path to salvation, which explains why universalism is so enticing.

The Gospel's Exclusive Claims

One of the dogmatic values of current American culture is pluralism: everything is plausibly acceptable. In religion this translates into the belief that there are many ways to God, that people can find their own spiritual path to eternity.

But the Bible does not allow for religious pluralism. There is one lord and he is Jesus. Four times in the New Testament Jesus is declared to be King of all kings and Lord of all lords (1 Timothy 6:15; Hebrews 7:1;

Revelation 17:14 and 19:16). In Acts 4:12 Luke proclaims, *There is salvation in no one else! God has given no other name under heaven by which we must be saved.* In John 14:6 Jesus told Thomas, *I am the way, the truth, and the life. No one can come to the Father except through me.*

This scandalously exclusive aspect of the Christian message is rooted in recognition of Jesus as the divine Son of God and his substitutionary atonement on the cross as the ultimate expression of God's love. As people struggle through their journey from unbelief to belief the confession "Jesus is Lord" is the turning point. There is no other way, no other message, no other person, no alternative religion. The statement "Jesus is Lord" is the breakthrough confession of faith.

A second implication of Mark's Great Commission is that we must communicate our belief in spoken words. Remember what Hybels said? "… we must know the gospel message cold and be ready to communicate it concisely and clearly … Without this, people are left guessing what it is that sets us apart in our quality of living."[2]

It has become popular among Christians to argue that practicing humanitarian activities of all sorts—feeding the poor, sheltering the homeless, healing the sick (and I do hope these sound both familiar and biblical to you)—is the same as proclaiming the gospel. We call these good works being the "hands and feet of Jesus" or "compassion evangelism." We might even quote Francis of Assisi. "Preach the gospel always, when necessary use words." It might surprise you to know that Francis, a powerful preacher, most likely never made this statement.[3]

This line of reasoning is incomplete. Unless and until we verbally, clearly, plainly tell the good news of Jesus, we cannot assume people have heard *or* experienced the gospel. The ultimate purpose of sharing faith is to provide people the opportunity to hear the gospel in a way that clearly and comprehensibly communicates to them the love of God so they can make a reasonable, informed decision about their relationship with God through Jesus Christ.

> PREACH THE GOSPEL—
> USE ACTIONS WHEN NECESSARY;
> USE WORDS ALWAYS.
>
> MARK GALLI[4]

The Consequences of the Gospel

The final point from Mark's account of the Great Commission concerns the consequences of the gospel. Of all the commission accounts, only Mark clearly describes the results of gospel preaching. Some will believe and be saved while others will disbelieve and be condemned.

This is a hard point to make, so black and white. The reason shar-

2. Hybels & Mittelberg, Kindle Edition, 46.
3. Mark Galli, *Francis of Assisi and His World* (Wastmont, IL: InterVarsity, 2003).
4. "Speak the Gospel," christianitytoday.com/ct/2009/mayweb-only/120-42.0.html?start=2 (May 21, 2009).

ing our faith is so important is that there are lost people. The very idea of saying someone is lost is difficult for us. To say they would be condemned for eternity is so ... permanent, so judgmental. Doesn't it make God look bad? Who wants to believe in a God who would eternally punish someone? It's as bad as believing in a God who would allow the sickness of a broken world to take the lives of innocent children. Do you feel the tension of where Mark takes us?

This tension of eternal judgment is so strong that a specific theological viewpoint, universalism, was developed to release the tension. Universalism takes different forms, but a consistent theme is that God will not hand down eternal punishment. Whether after a time of purgatory, a period in hell, or after some sort of soul sleep, universalists believe God will say "enough is enough." He will extend salvation to all people, through Christ, regardless of whether or not they professed faith in life.

The Gospel of Mark provides us with "one of the most controversial, brief, and foundational statements of the Great Commission."[4] He points us to the task of preaching, the potency of sharing faith and the urgency of belief in Jesus as Lord. According to Mark 16:16, those who believe and are baptized will be saved while those who fail to believe will be condemned. The reality of hell looms large in matters of belief.

Jesus' story makes us question whether condemnation to hell was merely an illustration or if it was a spiritual reality Jesus saw. Apparently he recognized a radical difference between those who would be saved and those who would be condemned. The dividing line between the two was belief. To describe this divide, Jesus gave the vivid illustration of the beggar Lazarus and the rich man (Luke 16:19-31).

Reading: Hybels, Chapters 5-6

In chapter 5 Hybels addresses one of the theological dilemmas that cycles through Christian history—how compassion is related to evangelism. Each of these concepts is a biblical imperative. But is there a priority where either evangelism or compassion is more significant than the other or is there a coterminous relationship where evangelism and compassion exist in symbiotic relationship with each other?

Explain how you see the relationship between evangelism and compassion.

_____

_____

_____

_____

_____

_____

---

4. William Banks, *Great Commission*, 67.

This question is significant because we often view compassion and evangelism as existing on a single continuum. We feel a tension between the two and with that tension comes a sense of guilt. It's as if we have to compromise by focusing on one or the other—as if we are constantly trying to find a balance between them.

What if instead of a single continuum (diagram 1) there are actually two continuums where both have a low and high end (diagram 2)? Diagram 2 is the model Hybels works from. There is a low and a high for both evangelism and compassion.

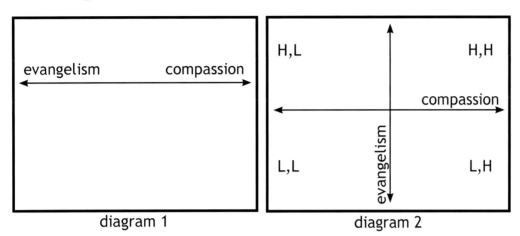

diagram 1   diagram 2

Here's how we can think about the relationship between compassion and evangelism. A compassionate lifestyle should be a result of Christian faith. God had compassion on us and so we have compassion on others (Matthew 18:12-35). God's compassion is expressed in its ultimate form through the gospel, the story of Jesus. Our lives of compassion are not a bait and switch maneuver to suck people into a gospel presentation. Rather, we are compassionate because we are living out the nature of God. Because of that compassionate nature we lovingly speak of God's ultimate compassion through the life of Jesus.

How do you see compassion and evangelism working together?

_____

_____

_____

_____

Hybels keeps on challenging us to develop a high potency Christian life as he takes us to sacrifice in chapter 6.

Of the three types of sacrifice Hybel's mentions—time, money, and modeling—which do you feel is your strongest, most natural way of sacrificing? Why do you say that?

_____

_____

_____

Often we find ourselves counting our sacrifices in relationships that are close to us: family, friends, and church people. How can you use your prime method of sacrificing on behalf of people who are not believers?

_____

_____

_____

_____

_____

Who Are God's Lost People?

We're going to focus our attention here on the first generation of twenty-first century adults, the Millennial generation. This is the name given to the seventy-eight million people born between 1980 and 2000, the largest generation in America's history.[5] Thom and Jess Rainer published research on this generation in their book *The Millenials*. Here are the basic facts they reported:

- Millennials believe they can do something great and they want it to matter.

- Relationships are everything to them.

- They are learners.

- Religion, specifically Christianity, is not on their radar screen.

When a Millennial says Christianity is not on her radar screen, she represents the eighty-seven percent of Millenials who place religion of any kind low on their list of priorities and the twenty-eight percent who claim no religious belief system of any kind.[6]

I am writing these words as I sit in the common room of the Florence Academy of Art in Moindal, Sweden, where my son is studying portrait painting. There are seventeen students and five faculty here this trimester. During my stay I've had the opportunity to talk with most of these people on a variety of topics, including conversations about their faith beliefs and practices.

While many of the students here are from Scandinavian countries where Christianity has already become a dead option (in Sweden only eight percent of people claim to be Christians and only one percent attend religious services), a few, including Hannah, are from America. When I asked Hannah if she was a believer she wrinkled up her nose, shook her head, and said, "No, I don't believe in anything." Christianity is not on Hannah's radar screen. For her at this point, it's not even an option.

---

5. Thom S. Rainer and Jess W. Rainer, *The Millennials* (Nashville: B&H Publishing, 2010), Kindle Edition, Location 238 and following.
6. Rainer, *Millennials*, Kindle Location 3332.

In the Portland, Oregon, area we talk about the 3G people. By 3G we mean third generation. When I meet these people and faith comes into our conversation they will very quickly say, "My grandparents were Christians of the _____ church. My parents quit going to church and I have never been part of a church."

It's not fair, nor helpful, to think that Millennials are all the same in their level of unbelief. In his earlier work, *The Unchurched Next Door*, Thom Rainer identified five levels of unbelief that he turned into what he named the U-scale, where U stands for Unchurched.[7]

- **U5 - Antagonistic**. A person who is a U5 does not like Christianity. This person is vocally antagonistic. Any talk about faith will be angry talk.

- **U4 - Resistant**. A person who is a U4 may be resistant to anything religious or may be generally religious with a specific resistance to Christianity. A U4 will generally avoid talking about faith or religion. Hannah is a U4.

- **U3 - Neutral**. A person who is a U3 is the most slippery in the scale to get a handle on. U3s tend to be neutral in their views, with leanings either away from faith (U4) or towards faith (U2). They often will engage in spiritual conversations.

- **U2 - Receptive**. A person who is a U2 falls into the "seeker" category. This person is not a believer but is looking. A U2 may have some knowledge about Christianity but it is usually a strange mix of ideas. A U2 is typically approachable and responsive to invitations to consider Christian faith.

- **U1 - Highly Receptive**. A U1 is ready to make a decision but may not know how. A U1 may be confused about major points of Christianity. When I was sixteen two guys in their early twenties were following the Rolling Stones concert tour selling Mick Jagger tongue t-shirts. They walked into our church worship service asking, "We've been reading the Bible and it talks about being baptized if you want to be saved. Do you guys baptize here?" That's a U1!

The following chart shows how the different U types are distributed across the US population. The dotted line represents the divide between those with whom faith conversations are more and less difficult to have.

---

7. Thom S. Rainier, *The Unchurched Next Door* (Grand Rapids: Zondervan, 2003).

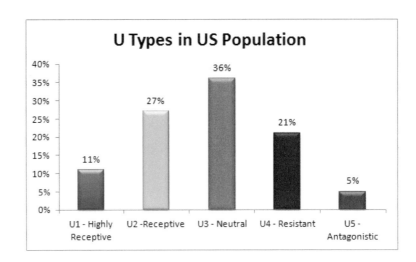

Almost three out of four people you meet in your city and community are potentially open to having a genuine spiritual conversation. See if you can name a person you already know in each of these U categories.

- U1 _____
- U2 _____
- U3 _____
- U4 _____
- U5 _____

Three-Question Conversations

She was a fiftyish, red-headed waitress in the Noshville Delicatessen in Nashville, Tennessee. Gena and I were meeting some friends there for lunch. We noticed her red hair first, then her Scottish brogue—not the normal Nashville accent! We asked the obvious question about her accent and where she was from. The next obvious question was how long she had been in the States and in Nashville.

As we ordered lunch I told her we were going to have a prayer for our food and was there anything we could pray about for her? That was our third question. She was so startled she almost ran back to the kitchen. We knew she had to return to bring our lunch plates to us. When she did she began to tell us her story until finally she said, "If you could pray for my son and I as we try to decide whether to fly back to Scotland to visit my son's father who is dying of cancer. He was once my husband but we've been separated so long now I only see him as my son's father."

Here was an immigrant in Nashville, talking to perfect strangers, telling us the most important question she had in her life at the time. Why would she do that? Why would she open herself up to us?

For many of us, it is scary to talk with people about Jesus. If it weren't scary many more of us would be having many more faith-oriented conversations with our friends, neighbors, and others. There is a way for you to get over your fear—practice! You need to practice talking to people in a way that allows faith to be shared in a natural, acceptable way. Some find it easier to practice first with strangers. Some prefer to start with friends. You should find what works best for you.

Here's how I want you to practice. The process I used with our Noshville Delicatessen waitress is what I've termed the "Three Question Conversation." You can use this process absolutely anywhere, anytime. My wife's favorite place to use it is in the checkout line at the grocery story. There are three types of questions in this conversation, the Polite Question, the Interest Question, and the Caring Question.

Here's how the Three Question Conversation works.

The Polite Question

When we meet someone, we typically ask a polite question such as, "How are you?" This is a safe, socially expected question that is typically answered by another safe, socially acceptable statement. "Fine, thank you." This all occurs in what is called the "public sphere." The Polite Question is neutral in content and does not call for any significant or meaningful contact with the other person. It has a low emotional content. The trick is to not stop at this first question but to move on to the second and third questions.

The Interest Question

This question should be something that is relevant to the situation. If you're standing in line at the grocery store it could be, "Do you shop here often?" If it's at a sporting event with your children an obvious question is, "Which child are you here with?" If it's related to school it could be, "How is your child's school going?" The Interest Question has two important effects. One, it demonstrates that you have an interest in the other person. Since most people stop at the Polite Question, the Interest Question is different. It catches people's attention. Two, it serves as a transition question. It moves the conversation from the public sphere to the private sphere. When you ask this second question you are telling the other person that you are interested in them (you are, right?) and you are offering a point of connection.

The Caring Question

The Caring Question signals to the other person that you are not only interested in them, but you care about them. Before you ask the Caring Question, share something about yourself. If you've asked who their child is on the ball field, point out your own child. Add an extra piece of information such as your child's name, school, or how long your child has been on the team. If you've asked about their child at school, share something about your child at school. This extra information helps establish you as a safe person, which is important in our on-guard, stranger danger society. After you've shared something personal, ask your third question.

The Polite Question and Interest Question stuck to the facts. Make your Caring Question about feelings. "Are you feeling good about your child's experience?" or "Do you feel like this is a good environment?"

When you ask the Caring Question, be prepared to hear something amazing. People may tell you some of the most intimate and life-challenging pieces of information. I've had people tell me about divorces, run-away children, terminal illnesses, and more. Why would people do this? Why would strangers almost rush to share these intimate details about their lives with you? I can think of two reasons. First, few people today actually listen to others. People are surprised by and hungry for a listening ear. Second, people no longer have safe places to talk about the deep issues of life. We aren't supposed to get personal at work. Homes are often places of emotional trauma. Friendships are often built around fun. Pushing to a deeper level with friends can endanger the relationship or open up opportunities for betrayal.

WHEN SHARING FAITH, MOVE THE CONVERSATION FROM THE PUBLIC SPHERE TO THE PRIVATE SPHERE.

The more you practice the Three Question Conversation, the more natural it will feel to you and the easier your Caring Question will come.

Ending the Three Question Conversation

When you practice the Three Question Conversation, be prepared to spend time with people. It may take five, ten, or even thirty minutes to have the whole discussion. These conversations can also lead to second meetings. (We'll discuss those later.) For now, end the Three Question Conversation with a statement of faith. You are taking the time to have these conversations because the love of Christ indwells you. You genuinely care for the people you engage in conversation. You are interested in their lives and their faith. Before you part ways with someone, bless him with a God encounter.

1. Thank him—profusely—for sharing with you. He has entrusted you with a precious gift of personal insight into his life. By thanking him you openly receive and acknowledge his gift. Your thanks is a blessing in and of itself, but don't stop there.

2. Make some statement that brings up God, Jesus, or faith. Here's an example of a short, powerful statement, "You are so courageous, I pray that God gives you strength to continue to meet this challenge." This both affirms the person and serves as a prayer on his behalf. That's right, a prayer. In public. You didn't need to bow your heads, hold hands, close your eyes, or even say Amen. Those things can come later. These few words are a powerful prayer that acknowledge you are a believer. They confirm that you do care and are demonstrating your care in a way that makes sense to you. It also affirms that you believe God is the one at work in his life.

3. Swap names. If you haven't already done so, share your first and last name with the person and get his first and last name. After you've parted ways write down both names so you can pray deliberately for this person later. First names are public sphere and last names are private sphere. When you get someone's last name you have taken a step towards a relationship.

You'll notice I'm not asking you to get into a biblical discussion. You're not talking about faith, repentance, baptism, or any of the gospel details at this point. You are establishing yourself as a believer who is interested in this other person. You are helping people feel good about Jesus followers and faith. You are cultivating their hearts for more encounters with God. You may not be the person who eventually gets to share Jesus with this person. You are one of God's influences that he is putting into that person's life as he guides them towards himself.

Action Step

This week begin practicing the Three Question Conversation. Set a goal for the week for how many people you want to practice this with. If you're a more reserved person one conversation a week may be the place to start. If you're an outgoing person who loves interacting with new people, one conversation a day might be more appropriate for you.

Reporting

Turn to Lesson 4 in your Personal Answer Book and complete these exercises.

Missional Director Meeting

Schedule your second meeting with your missional director.

Lesson 5: Why People Don't Believe

Is it harder for people to become Christians today than twenty or thirty years ago? This question is difficult to answer. Consider these findings from the Pew Forum's 2008 U.S. Religious Landscape Survey of 35,000 Americans age eighteen and older:

- More than a quarter (28%) of American adults reported having left the faith in which they were raised for no faith or another faith tradition.

- 44% have switched religious affiliation, either from no faith tradition to one, or from a faith tradition to no faith.

- The number of people who report no religious affiliation as adults (16.1%) is twice the number who report no religious affiliation as children.

- Among 18-29 year olds a quarter say they are not currently affiliated with any particular religion. This is nine percentage points higher than in the overall adult population.[8]

Now how would you answer the question, "Is it harder for people to become Christians today than twenty or thirty years ago?"

_____

_____

_____

_____

_____

Reading: Hybels, Chapters 7-9

Among the perennial issues of modern American society are loneliness and social disconnectedness. Jacqueline Olds and Richard Schwartz, in their book *The Lonely American*, describe some of the forces that feed American isolation. These forces include two income work demands, overly busy schedules, and social technologies.[9] These external factors feed into underlying American attitudes of individualism, self-reliance and self-centeredness. The result is a culture that builds isolation and breaks apart community.

Hybels asks a simple question to expose the weaknesses of this type of culture. "Where do you go when you have a problem?"

You may have felt uncomfortable with chapters seven and eight, not

---

8. *U.S. Religious Landscape Survey: Summary of Key Findings.* Washington: The Pew Forum on Religion & Public Life (2008), 5, 7. Available at: http://religions. pewforum.org/reports.

9. Jacqueline Olds and Richard S. Schwartz, *The Lonely American: Drifting Apart in the Twenty First Century* (Boston: Beacon, 2009).

because they're difficult, but because your "authenticity" detectors are set on maximum. These chapters may have made you feel that Hybels is only encouraging you to develop relationships so you can later invite people into a Jesus conversation, the "bait and switch" routine again.

What is the difference between an authentic personal encounter and an inauthentic one?

For me, the difference is genuine care. When I meet people and begin asking them questions, I first have to do a gut check. Do I genuinely care about this person?

What barriers tend to keep you from building relationships with people?

_____

_____

_____

_____

_____

_____

_____

The Matthew Party idea Hybels presents in chapter eight became famous and well-used when this book first came out. Hybels revived it in a sermon series in May 2012. His idea is to deliberately plan life in ways that incorporate connecting points with other people. He says we should plan "relaxed time together outside of the routines of work, household chores, or the everyday busyness of life" (p. 109).

For some, these connecting activities are as natural as breathing. (If your Myers-Briggs/Golden personality type has an E or F, this may be you). For others this is difficult. (Someone with an I or T in their personality type may not find connecting activities natural.)

It's important to not let yourself go on a guilt trip. Also, don't give the easy excuse, "it's not my personality type." Instead, dial this into who you are. Some people have huge networks of friends and relationships. Others have much smaller networks. No matter what size your relationship networks are, you do have them.

Action Step

With the ideas from these Hybels chapters in mind go to lesson 5 of your Personal Answer Book and write your list of people who are in each of Hybels' network categories. These are people you would like to see drawn into a closer relationship with Jesus and a community of faith. They may be non-religious, they may be disconnected from church, dissatisfied or even "there but not involved."

This list gives you your prayer focus. Share the names with your

prayer group. Ask them to start praying weekly, if not more often, over these people. You need to pray at least weekly for them as well. Ask God to reveal to you his intents for them, what you need to know about them, and words to begin a conversation of faith with them.

Cultural Defeater Beliefs

DEFEATER
BELIEF: A
CULTURALLY-
BASED DOUBT
GENERATOR

Tim Keller, founding planter and lead minister of Redeemer Presbyterian Church in New York City and one of the leading apologists for Christianity Today, answers our question about whether it is difficult to become a Christian today with an unqualified yes! It is definitely harder for people to become a Christian today than it was 20 years ago. Keller argues that under Christendom[10] (when the Christian faith was recognized as the dominant religious and cultural force), culture worked in favor of Christian belief. In our post-Christendom world, cultural forces work against Christian belief through what Keller calls defeater beliefs.

A defeater belief is a "culturally-based doubt generator." Keller says, "Every culture hostile to Christianity holds to a set of 'common sense' consensus beliefs that automatically make Christianity seem implausible to people. These are what philosophers call 'defeater beliefs.' A defeater belief is *Belief A* that, if true, means *Belief B* can't be true."[11]

What are some of America's cultural defeater beliefs? Keller uses some defeater beliefs as chapter titles in his book *The Reason for God: Belief in the Age of Skepticism.*[12]

- There Can't Be Just One True Religion

- How Could a Good God Allow Suffering?

- The Church is Responsible for So Much Injustice

- Science Has Disproved Christianity

How have you experienced the influence of defeater beliefs? You could have your own doubts, or they may be espoused by someone you know.

_____

_____

_____

_____

---

10. An excellent resource is *A Resurrected Church: Christianity After the Death of Christendom* by Charles H. Bayer (Chalice Press, 2001).

11. Tim Keller, "Deconstructing Defeater Beliefs: Leading the Secular to Christ." Available at: churchleaders.com/outreach-missions/free-resources-outreach-missions/157981-free-ebooklet-deconstructing-defeater-beliefs-by-tim-keller.html

12. Riverhead Trade, 2009.

A set of widely held defeater beliefs begins working as a culture's worldview system, creating what Keller terms an implausibility structure. The result is cultural hostility towards Christianity. It is this well-formed implausibility structure that makes evangelism more difficult and complex today than it was twenty or thirty years ago. In today's cultural worldview, Christianity appears ludicrous so why put any effort into investigating it?

Dealing With Cultural Defeater Beliefs

How do we deal with these cultural defeater beliefs and the implausibility structure they create that convinces people Christianity is not worth their effort?

Keller suggests we engage in deconstructing these defeater beliefs. Deconstructing means getting to the center of the issue where assumptions begin to unravel, where the negative beliefs no longer hold together as a coherent model for life.

While the idea of deconstructing defeater beliefs is complex, the approach is actually a fairly simple three-step process.

1. Start the conversation of faith with a vivid, attractive Christian perspective that is so compelling, the listener says, "It would be wonderful if that were true."

One of the best ways to do this is to share an experience, share something you have learned (or are learning), or share a point of Christian life you are struggling to practice.

We have new friends who have been becoming Christians for several years now. They've been living together for a number of years. Both were previously married or living with someone. She is a fairly new believer. He is not a believer yet. As part of their exploration of Christianity, they made the decision to get married. At their wedding a former co-worker of the bride asked my wife how this wedding had come about. My wife explained their situation in more detail than I have here. She mentioned their process of making new decisions based on Jesus.

The woman's response was, "She's done that, been living like this and now you're giving her a wedding? I've never heard of a church like this! Who are you?"

We help the unbeliever see something so compelling that it overcomes her natural apathy towards Christianity. We bring to the surface a longing for something more, different, better.

2.   Be able to state the defeater belief the person is feeling more clearly, more accurately, more convincingly than they can.

In our wedding example it might go like this:

"I understand your shock. Church people so often come across as prejudiced, bigoted people who live in a black and white world where you're either in or out, saved or damned. But you know, this woman is convinced God has a better life for her so she's trying it out, and that's what we're all trying to do in this church."

By being able to state clearly and boldly what she is thinking we develop credibility. Obviously, to state this defeater belief so strongly must mean we've thought about it, maybe even more than she has.

3. Provide a longer explanation of the Christian perspective.

This is a more subtle process than Keller describes. I explain step three as a "listening conversation." Step one gets the person's attention. Step two gives you credibility. Step three allows you to demonstrate you are a safe person. Remember, you're still breaking down defeater belief stereotypes. A listening conversation is one that invites questions and comments, asks new questions, and listens. In the process of listening you make the attitude of Jesus—his heart—the primary object and sprinkle the truth of Jesus lightly.

People today are thirsty for Jesus' heart. That is what they fall in love with. Many of the truths of Jesus' teachings come later in people's journey toward trusting him.

Conducting a Spiritual Diagnosis

When you are sick and go to the doctor, the doctor takes your medical history before doing a diagnosis. The doctor needs to know what's wrong with you before prescribing a course of treatment. Any other approach would be silly. In the same way, you need to learn how to do spiritual diagnoses before helping people take their next steps of faith.

When Jesus met the Samaritan woman at the well in John 4, he made an insightful spiritual diagnosis. What an engaging conversation they had! Jesus started small by asking for a drink. When they got into religion, things heated up. Ultimately Jesus delved into her personal life and life-style choices. Talk about confrontation! But the conversation changed her life. In John 4:39, she said, "He told me everything I ever did!"

When you do a spiritual diagnosis, you are listening for the reasons a person does not believe. These reasons for unbelief can be grouped into four main categories.

Reasons for Unbelief

1. Intellectual. Keller's defeater beliefs fall into this category along with other intellectual objections.

- Science Has Disproved Christianity
- How Could a Good God Allow Suffering?
- The Church is Responsible for So Much Injustice

2. Life-Style. People do make life-style choices that may prohibit belief. Sometimes they choose these life-styles to demonstrate unbelief. Life-style choices are often sensitive topics, involving choices of sexual behavior, dress, activities, and even professions.

3. Oppression. Oppression includes events such as family of origin issues, dependencies, addictions, and even personality disorders and personal traumas. There is a distinct difference between life-style and oppression. Where life-style issues are choices people make, oppressions are outside their control. Those who grew up in an abusive home environment had no choice in how they were treated but they bear deep scars that may harden them against faith in God.

4. Bad Experiences. Two kinds of bad experiences are involved here. The first are bad life experiences. We live in a broken world in which bad things happen to people, like when someone loses a child to a devastating illness and they cannot let that event go. The second kind of bad experiences are bad encounters with Christians. It is a continual wonder to hear stories of how people have been mistreated by those who profess faith in Jesus.

In conducting a spiritual diagnosis, you are a listener. As you talk with people, move the conversation towards a spiritual topic and listen to the other person. In your head, go through the list of main reasons people don't believe and try to identify which one best fits this person.

The diagram shows the flow of sharing faith. Start with spiritual diagnosis so you know where the person is. Then introduce Jesus into the conversation. You can find a story of Jesus that connects with each of the main reasons people do not believe.

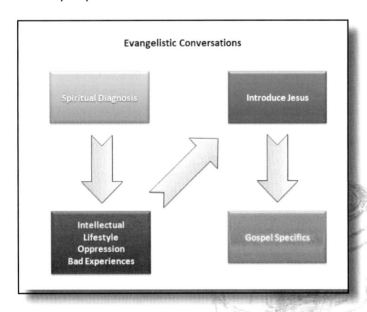

- Nicodemus's religious understanding kept him from believing Jesus. (John 3)
- The Samaritan woman 's life-style stood in her way. (John 4)
- The blind man experienced physical oppression. (John 9)
- The woman caught in adultery was mistreated by religious people. (John 8)

41

These stories become connecting points in people's lives. Once they begin to see Jesus and gain some sense of how Jesus desires to interact with them, the faith conversation can deepen. We want them to experience Jesus and be drawn to him. Once that happens we can begin to share gospel specifics.

A word of caution. This process may run counter to how you were taught. I was taught that the "gospel comes by hearing the word of God" (Rom. 10:17). The common interpretation of this scripture several decades ago meant the correct starting point was with gospel specifics. This approach may have worked a generation ago. It seldom works now.

By this point in the module you should be more aware of the people around you. Your curiosity about people should be growing. You should be wondering about people's stories and their faith journeys. You should also be more engaged in prayer over the people you are meeting. Do you have a growing prayer list for people? Are you writing down their names and details, perhaps in a journal or a 3x5 card file?

In the next lesson you will transition from chance, random encounters with people through the Three Question Conversations to more planned, deliberate conversations with the three categories of people who are already in your relationship network.

Action Step

Turn to Lesson 5 in your Personal Answer Book. Look at the spiritual diagnosis section. Your assignment is to have a conversation with one of the people on your list and conduct a spiritual diagnosis.

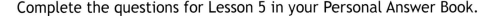

Reporting

Complete the questions for Lesson 5 in your Personal Answer Book.

Unit C
Conversion

Author and progressive political activist Anne Lamott[1] is one of the better known—and controversial—Christian converts of our generation. Lamott was raised as an atheist by parents who were fully immersed in the philosophical "implausibility structures" of America. In the Lamott family, belief in Christianity was right up there with belief in E.T. (1982).

In her book *Traveling Mercies*[2] Lamott wondrously relates the emotional journey of her conversion in 1984 in the tiny St. Andrew Presbyterian Church in Marin City, California. At the time she was 30 years old, trying to write by day and drinking herself into oblivion at night. Her typical Sunday morning regimen was "hungover or coming down off a cocaine binge," to wander through the Sausalito Flea Market. One Sunday she noticed gospel music coming from a church across the street. At home, later that day, she relates:

Anne Lamott

After a while, as I lay there, I became aware of someone with me, hunkered down in the corner, and I just assumed it was my father, whose presence I had felt over the years when I was frightened and alone. The feeling was so strong that I actually turned on the light for a moment to make sure no one was there —of course, there wasn't. But after a while, in the dark again, I knew beyond any doubt that it was Jesus. I felt him as surely as I feel my dog lying nearby as I write this.

And I was appalled... I thought about what everyone would think of me if I became a Christian, and it seemed an utterly impossible thing that simply could not be allowed to happen. I turned to the wall and said out loud, "I would rather die."

I felt Him just sitting there on His haunches in the corner of my sleeping loft, watching me with patience and love, and I squinched my eyes shut, but that didn't help because that's not what I was seeing Him with. Finally I fell asleep, and in the morning, He was gone ...

And one week later, when I went back to church, I was so hungover that I couldn't stand up for the songs, and this time I stayed for the sermon, which I just thought was so ridiculous, like someone trying to convince me of the existence of extraterrestrials, but the last song was so deep and raw and pure that I could not escape. It was as if the people were singing in between the notes, weeping and joyful at the same time, and I felt like their voices or something was rocking me in

---

1. Photo source: http://topics.nytimes.com/topics/reference/timestopics/people/l/anne_lamott/index.html
2. *Traveling Mercies* (New York: Anchor, 2000), 44-50.

its bosom, holding me like a scared kid, and I opened up to that feeling—and it washed over me.

I began to cry and left before the benediction, and I raced home and felt the little cat running at my heels, and I walked down the dock past dozens of potted flowers, under a sky as blue as one of God's own dreams, and I opened the door to my houseboat, and I stood there a minute, and then I hung my head and said... "I quit." I took a long deep breath and said out loud, "All right. You can come in."

So this was my beautiful moment of conversion.

Conversion in the faith-debilitating atmosphere created by the defeater beliefs of America is seldom a single "light shining forth" experience. In fact, conversion itself is a rare event. Like Lamott's conversion, belief in and acceptance of Christ often arrives via a series of experiences and mini-decisions through which the person tries out faith, seeking to come to grips with the life implications of opening up to Jesus.

In this unit we will look at conversion. What is conversion? How does it happen? What conversion pathways do people typically follow? How do we help people along their conversion path? This is an exciting topic, one that will enrich and empower your personal spiritual discipline of sharing faith.

Lesson 6: Understanding Conversion

I grew up with a very naive concept of conversion. My faith heritage assumed that conversion was pretty much a point action event that happened based upon intellectual knowledge. When a person properly understood the gospel, that Jesus is Lord and baptism is necessary for forgiveness of sins, we took that person to the water and—voila!—they were a Christian.

With age and experience, my view of conversion has changed. I pray that I treat people with more insight now. Conversion is a multi-layered process that moves deeper and deeper into a person's life, changing what they think, how they act, and even why they feel the way they do. As the Hebrews writer says, when the word of God works in a person's life, it is sharper than a two-edged sword (4:12).

Great Commission

Matthew 28:18-20—Divine Authority

In 1844 near Rhymney, England, a small riot erupted. A wagon was attacked, pandemonium broke loose in the local chapel, and a lot of tobacco juice was spit in the faces of the "other side" as the heated crowd drew lines for and against.[3] What was the spark that ignited the chaos? It was baptism. They were fighting over whether infants of believers should be baptized and if immersion (water dunking) was the right mode of baptism.

Matthew 28:18-20 is the quintessential expression of the Great Commission. These verses were what we memorized in Sunday school, what we recited on stage in front of beaming family, and often the motivating command for propelling missionaries into strange and sometimes dangerous places.

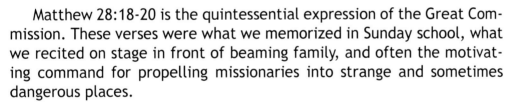

Then Jesus came to them and said, "All authority in heaven and on earth has been given to me. Therefore go and make disciples of all nations, baptizing them in the name of the Father and of the Son and of the Holy Spirit, and teaching them to obey everything I have commanded you. And surely I am with you always, to the very end of the age."

In Matthew's commissioning record the death-risen Jesus announces his claim as the recipient of the divine authority of God. His universal lordship will now be expressed through a universal mission that includes both Israelite and Gentile. Those who are his disciples are to carry on his mission of kingdom: to make disciples. How do disciples make more disciples? By baptizing those who receive the word and teaching them the ways of life in their Lord Jesus.

To his disciples, and through them to us, the risen Lord Jesus commands his followers to be faith sharers and disciple makers. Through Christian history, obedience to this command has been a powerful mo-

---

3. David M. Thompson, *Baptism, Church, and Society in Modern Britain* (Waynesboro, GA: Paternoster, 2005), 114-115.

tivator for missions, preaching, and evangelizing. Yet the idea of command and obedience are not comfortable to many people today. We chaff against the idea of an authority figure telling us what to do. Yet here are other motivations that compel us as well.

For me, the command of Matthew 28 has been powerful. It was part of our motivation to do mission work in Kenya for ten years. But it is not my only motivation. I also believe that a Jesus follower has a better life right now, though not necessarily an easier one. I have seen deep suffering in the lives of very faithful, believing friends. But in the midst of their suffering Jesus dwells as their "balm of Gilead," their suffering servant who walks and talks with them in their garden of pain.

I also don't want people to go to hell. Now, there's a politically incorrect point of view. People today don't talk about hell, yet Ed Stetzer's research showed that sixty percent of 20-29 year olds believe there is a place of punishment called hell.[4]

What motivations do you feel in your life to share faith with your family, friends, neighbors, and others?

_____

_____

_____

_____

_____

_____

_____

Reading: Hybels, chapters 10-12

In these chapters Hybels gets to the heart of the matter—sharing faith!

How did you feel as your read the opening story of chapter 10 about Hybel's conversation with the Muslim cab driver?

_____

_____

_____

_____

_____

_____

---

4. Ed Stetzer, *Lost and Found: The Younger Unchurched and the Churches that Reach Them* (Nashville: B & H, 2009).

Of the three methods Hybels described, which one feels most natural to you?

❑ Direct

❑ Indirect

❑ Invitational Methods

As you think about these three approaches (and there are others as well), it is worth recognizing that your answer as to which feels most natural is made in the context of our cultural influences. Religion has been put on the "do not touch" list of American society. Defeater beliefs and the resulting implausibility structures make talk of faith, Jesus, and Christianity appear, as in Anne Lamott's story, like something from outer space. It sounds absurd.

Given these strong pushes against ever speaking about faith, do you think the method you marked above is your most natural method of raising conversations about faith? Or could you feel this way because you're uncomfortable, not confident, or because you don't have much experience? Reflect on this point and record your answer.

_____

_____

_____

_____

_____

_____

Hybels suggests—no, more than that, he makes a direct point—sharing faith is not a matter of convenience. It's a matter of obedience. Read the following two verses.

Always be prepared to give an answer to everyone who asks you to give the reason for the hope that you have. But do this with gentleness and respect (1 Pet. 3:15).

Preach the word; be prepared in season and out of season; correct, rebuke and encourage —with great patience and careful instruction (2 Tim. 4:2).

Are these really to be read as divine imperatives and not just gentle suggestions? If you accept these verses as direct commands, what implications do you see for yourself?

_____

_____

_____

_____

_____

_____

Sharing faith is intimidating because the people we share with don't take our faith at face value. They tend to ask questions, questions that can be difficult to answer. People need to wrestle with their doubts and unbelief. However, the intensity and topics of their questions can make us feel ill-prepared to share faith.

A book such as Lee Strobel's *Case for Faith*[5] is a thoughtful guide to help us think through barriers to belief. Even with this tool and others in hand, we don't need to have all the answers. In fact, being willing to say, "That's a great question and, honestly, I haven't thought about that particular question enough to give you a good answer," is good. It's an opportunity to be honest and to admit we don't know everything. It's also a great opportunity to say, "I'd really enjoy working on that question with you."

IF A COMMISSION BY AN EARTHLY KING IS CONSIDERED AN HONOR, HOW CAN A COMMISSION BY A HEAVENLY KING BE CONSIDERED A SACRIFICE?

— DAVID LIVINGSTONE

About Conversion

Conversion is a rare event in the life of any individual. Consider this: in America, only 15% of people will ever have a conversion experience, and this in the country with the second highest conversion percentage in the world![6] Lewis Rambo says the Mormons (the fastest growing religious group in America for the last thirty years) reported fewer than one conversion in every thousand connections. Conversions by the International Churches of Christ among people attending their evangelistic Bible talks was less than one person for every hundred.[7]

In a general social survey on conversions, the breakdown of conversion by age is as follows:

• 76% experienced their conversion before age 30.

• 15% were between 30 and 39.

• 9% were 40 or over.[8]

The motivations most associated with these religious conversions were:

• 37%—a change in marriage or family

• 25%—a change in social network or geographic location

• 18%—issues of theology

• 19%—other reasons[9]

---

5. Lee Strobel, *The Case for Faith: A Journalist Investigates the Toughest Objections to Christianity* (Grand Rapids, MI: Zondervan, 2000).

6. Robert J. Barro, Jason Hwang, and Rachel M. McCleary, "Religious Conversion in 40 Countries." *Journal for the Scientific Study of Religion,* Vol. 49:1 (2010), 15-36.

7. Lewis Rambo, *Understanding Religious Conversion* (New Haven, CT: Yale University Press, 1993).

8. General Social Survey, 1988. The GSS is widely regarded as the single best source of data on societal trends. Surveys have been conducted since 1972.

9. General Social Survey, 1988.

These facts changed my perspective on conversion from a somewhat rote process to an event of tender wonder. I now stand in awe before the baptistery as people express their commitment of faith in Jesus, considering what a rare and momentous process they are experiencing.

What insights do the above conversion facts bring to your mind?

_____

_____

_____

_____

_____

_____

Write Your Personal Conversion Story

The most confidence-inspiring preparation you can make for sharing faith in Jesus is to be able to tell your personal faith story. In *Permission Evangelism*[10] Michael Simpson stresses that ultimately, when the unbeliever has opened the opportunity for us to share with him, the best we can do is tell of the grace of the Lord's work and mercy in our own life.

Whether you grew up in a home where Christian faith was active or you became a believer as an adult, you have a story of God's love and influence in your life. One of my teachers at Fuller Theological Seminary's School of World Mission (now School of Intercultural Studies), Robert J. Clinton, powerfully influenced my understanding of my personal faith story by introducing me to four conversion patterns.

1. Heritage: The individual develops in the context of Christian faith and is more or less processed into Christian values and living. This is the kind of faith heritage expressed in Ephesians 6:1-3.

2. Radical Commitment: The individual develops in a non-Christian context into whatever values and lifestyle that context supports. Conversion involves learning Christian values and lifestyle. The Philippian jailer of Acts 16:16-34 is a biblical example.

3. Accelerated: This early and rapid developmental pattern occurs in the context of a family heritage of Christian faith. Timothy, whom Paul gathered into his traveling preaching group sometime in his teen years, is an example (2 Timothy 3:10-15).

4. Delayed: This describes the person who grows up in a faith heritage but rebels against that heritage until she eventually experiences conversion, which often leads to deep spiritual commitment. Paul is an example of this kind of conversion pattern (Acts 9:1-31).[11]

---

10. Michael L. Simpson, *Permission Evangelism* (Colorado Springs, CO: NexGen, 2004).

11. Robert J. Clinton, *Leadership Emergence Theory* (Altadena, CA: Barnabas

I'm using a carefully defined idea of conversion here: the time when the realization occurs that God should be placed as the centerpiece of life and a decision is made to pursue that ideal through new ways of living.[12] This is a directional definition of conversion, where one was facing away from Christ and now intentionally turns to move towards Christ. There are beginnings and culmination points in this conversion process that the definition does not make explicit, but it gives us a working understanding.

Of the four conversion patterns above, what is your conversion pattern?

_____

There are four elements to a conversion story: pre-decision life, process time, decision, and post-decision. Develop your story around these four elements and use the suggested percentages below for the amount of time you give to each element in your story.

Your Pre-decision Life (10%). Whatever your conversion pattern is, you had a time when it dawned on you that you were considering following Jesus. What happened before that time is your Pre-Christ material. Think about these items for this time period:

- Your context

- Significant people, events, and emotions

- Results on your life

Your Process Time (30%). This is when you began to see the light. If you had a radical conversion there may be some pretty dark times here. If you had a heritage conversion your process time may have been a gentle culmination. Think about these items for your process time:

- What questions, tensions or experiences brought you to the point you were willing to consider Jesus?

- Who or what helped you sort through these questions, tensions or experiences?

Decision (20%). Why did you make the commitment to believe and follow Jesus?

- What about Jesus was convincing, convicting, or compelling?

- What people were influential to your decision?

- What personal reflections were influential to your decision?

- What scripture ideas were foundational to your decision?

Resources, 1989), 342-347.
12. Annette Mahoney and Kenneth I. Pargament, "Sacred Changes: Spiritual Conversion and Transformation," *Journal of Clinical Psychology*, 60 (2004), 481-492.

Post-Decision (40%). How has your decision to follow Jesus impacted your life?

- What new state of mind did you receive?

- How has the decision impacted your relationships?

- How have you worked upon ongoing doubts or struggles?

- How has your decision to follow Jesus continued to influence your life decisions?

The left side of the following chart shows the way stories are typically told. The right side shows the way I am suggesting here. The typical story emphasizes the pre-decision life as a means to relate to the hearer. The result is there is little time spent on the movement towards Christ and the impact of Christ on your life. The suggested storyline offers enough pre-decision information to build a relationship with your listener, then emphasizes how you got to your decision and how Christ has since impacted your life. This orientation lets Christ become central to the story.[13] Zach Eswine says, "it spares the gory and raises the glory."[14]

"FAITH IS NOT BELIEF WITHOUT PROOF... BUT TRUST WITHOUT RESERVATION."
—ELTON TRUEBLOOD

Personal Story Elements

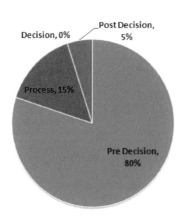

Typical Story

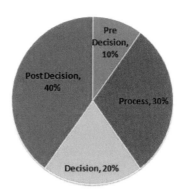

Suggested Story

---

13. Douglas M. Cecil, *The 7 Principles of an Evangelistic Life* (Chicago: Moody, 2003), 174.

14. Zack Eswine, *Preaching to a Post-Everything World* (Grand Rapids, MI: Baker, 2008).

Action Step

Use the outline suggested above and work on your personal conversion story. Don't feel you must slavishly answer each of the questions. Use them to guide you as you construct and polish your story.

Reporting

When you are done polishing your conversion story, turn to lesson 6 in your Personal Answer book and write it out.

Lesson 7:
Helping People Towards Conversion

The following story comes from one of our church planters in Oregon. This story demonstrates how deep unbelief can be.

My friend is a middle-aged divorced woman with one child. She is in all ways unremarkable in appearance, and in all ways intense, an incredibly intelligent swirling-storm-of-the-mind. She's a conflicted soul and confident of nothing whatsoever except that there cannot be a Hell, for if God lived up to his loving reputation he would surely find a way to overcome what separates anyone—including the Devil—from Himself.

My friend took years—literally—before she could muster the courage to approach me after a Chamber of Commerce breakfast just to introduce herself. We talked for 30 minutes or so, mainly her telling me how impossible it was that she would ever speak to me and how it was a minor miracle that she was doing so now, but how important it was that we all talk to one another.

She believes in God, so far as it goes, and believes God loves us, but says her first step to giving up on Christian faith was being unable to believe in Hell—"If there is nothing to be saved from there is no point in Christianity."

She is a blogger and an anonymous contributor to online discussions—including Oprah Winfrey's now-deleted forum, where her contributions often made the front page. She has been interviewed on Nightline in connection with her Oprah contributions. She has been involved in channeling, but is about done with that. Lately she has felt as much stringent legalism from New Age believers—if not more—than she ever knew in a church environment. "Now that I am not so edgy," she said, she plans to write a book presenting her questions from her life in skepticism. She has been quite harsh in her online life.

She obviously needed a listener from "my side of the chasm" who would not, in fact, cringe, condemn, or counterpoint. And she is convinced I am exceedingly rare in this regard. She mentioned the Alpha Course—how she was once invited—but is convinced she should stay away. Her motive—at least as far as she knows—seems to be to protect the naive and sheltered Christians hosting the course from ... herself.

I leave you with a quote she shared with me from her recent conversation with Portland radio talk show host Lars Larsen: "Everyone is an atheist of someone else's description of God."[15]

---

15. Story told by Wilson Parrish, church planter in Sherwood, OR.

The Great Commission

Matthew 28:18-20—Exploring Baptism

I come from the theological heritage of the American Restoration Movement, also known as the Stone-Campbell Movement. We are a trio of historically associated fellowships: Disciples of Christ, Churches of Christ, and Independent Christian Churches/Churches of Christ. We share the Anabaptist practice of adult believers' baptism by immersion. For us baptism is one of the essential practices that define Christian faith and life.

In my childhood years baptism was a major and perennial point of discussion and controversy. We asked questions such as, "Can someone be saved without being baptized?", "At what point is someone saved?" and "Is baptism effective if someone does not know it is for the remission of sins or is not baptized in the name of Jesus?" Our beliefs on baptism were not just distinctive, they were divisive. Rather than being a covenant sign of union with God in Christ, baptism was portrayed as the sundering act separating those of us with truth from all the rest who did not see things the same way we did.

Today I see a remarkable convergence in the Christian world around baptism. At the Exponential Conference in 2010 Irwin McManus used Acts 2:38 as his text for the final keynote speech. The Mars Hill church in Seattle practices baptism as one of the central sacraments of Christian faith. Among my Baptist friends, counting the raised hands of those who have prayed the sinner's prayer is no longer the numeric standard of faith. They now count immersions.

Despite this coalescing around baptism, many in the restoration fellowship are still uncomfortable with this topic. We struggle to maintain a sense of the nature of baptism while distancing ourselves from the appearance of judgmentalism, lest we come across as pronouncing salvation or damnation on others based on whether or how they were baptized.

What are your experiences or thoughts on baptism?

_____

_____

_____

_____

_____

What is baptism?

Baptism is a Christian practice. James Brownson, writing from the Calvinist, Reformed perspective, describes baptism as " an action or ritual or set of behaviors that Christians engage in to articulate, embody, and live out the gospel."[16] Brownson argues that Christian baptism is important, even central, to the Christian faith.

I like the way John Mark Hicks and Greg Taylor describe baptism as "an effectual sign," that is "a sign that actually effects what it symbolizes.[17] In Romans 6:5-6, Paul argued that through baptism we became part of the Jesus story as we mimicked his death and resurrection through the enacting event of baptism. What happened to Christ also happens to us as we die and are resurrected with Christ in baptism.[18]

We were therefore buried with him through baptism into death in order that, just as Christ was raised from the dead through the glory of the Father, we too may live a new life. If we have been united with him in a death like his, we will certainly also be united with him in a resurrection like his (Romans 6:5-6).

Paul's use of a burial metaphor raises the question of the mode of baptism. Is Christian baptism sprinkling or immersion? There are ages of debate over this question. Howard Marshall describes baptism as "the ceremony of Christian initiation whose central feature was this ritual using of water (generally understood to be originally by dipping or immersion), so that the word referred to the ceremony as a whole instead of the mere action with water."[19]

What does baptism do?

There are two big "baptism" camps in the Christian world. On one side are those who claim baptismal regeneration, that someone must be baptized to be saved. Baptismal regeneration is held by several historic faith traditions such as the Roman Catholic, Orthodox and Anglican churches. This view is supported through scriptures such as 1 Peter 3:21.

... and this water symbolizes baptism that now saves you also—not the removal of dirt from the body but the pledge of a clear conscience toward God. It saves you by the resurrection of Jesus Christ ...

In the other camp are those who claim a "faith only" stance. Many Protestant Evangelical churches hold this stance. Mark Driscoll of the Reformed tradition gave a classic formulation of the faith only position when he wrote, "We believe the Bible presents baptism as an outward witness of an inward faith in Jesus Christ alone for salvation. Christian baptism is an act of obedience to the command of Jesus, declaring the believers' faith in and identification with their crucified, buried, and

16. James V. Brownson, *The Promise of Baptism: An Introduction to Baptism in Scripture and the Reformed Tradition* (Grand Rapids, MI: Eerdmans, 2007), 37.

17. John Mark Hicks and Greg Taylor, *Down in the River to Pray* (Siloam Springs, AR: Leafwood, 2004), 250.

18. Brownson, 48.

19. Howard Marshall, "The Meaning of the Verb 'Baptize,'" in *Dimensions of Baptism: Biblical and Theological Studies,* 8-24, and Stanley Porter and Anthony R. Cross, eds., (London: Sheffield Academic Press, 2002), 9.

risen Savior. It is a visible declaration of the gospel of Jesus Christ."[20]

The "faith only" position is supported by such verses as Ephesians 2:8-9.

For it is by grace you have been saved, through faith—and this is not from yourselves, it is the gift of God—not by works, so that no one can boast.

IN BAPTISM WE ARE INITIATED INTO HIS CHURCH WHERE WE BEGIN TO LOOK AND ACT LIKE CHRIST.

The difference between these two theological perspectives is that the baptismal regeneration perspective says that baptism is an act *for* salvation while the "faith only" perspective says baptism is an act of obedience *because of* salvation.[21]

Regardless of which perspective you take, there are three primary results that the believer receives from baptism.

1. Baptism as cleansing (Acts 2:38, 22:16, Eph.5:25-26).

In the New Testament world baptism and cleansing (sin forgiveness) are inseparably linked.[22] This linkage between baptism and cleansing centers around blood. In the Old Testament, God extended his mercy towards his people on the Day of Atonement. The blood of animals was the activating agent (Lev. 16:15-19). In the New Testament this same linkage occurs through the blood of Jesus (1 Jn. 1:7, 1 Pet. 1:2; Heb. 10:1-18). "In the logic of the Bible, to be baptized into Christ's death is also to be sprinkled with Christ's blood."[23]

2. Baptism as initiation into the body of Christ, the church (1 Cor. 12:12-13, Gal. 3:27).

In baptism God seals us into union with Jesus. We are initiated into his church where we begin to look and act like Christ.[24] Hicks and Taylor describe the results of this inclusion as a new identity, a new ethic, and a new worldview (Col. 3:1-15).[25] Through baptism we begin to look like Jesus because we are dwelling in him (Rom. 8:9). Baptism is the event at which we are publicly welcomed into the visible church, the body of Christ, where our lives are slowly and sometimes painstakingly put back into order.

3. Baptism to receive the Holy Spirit (Acts 2:38, Rom. 8:9).

A person cannot be a Christian without also having received the Holy Spirit (Rom 8:9). The conversion stories of Acts are inconsistent about any normative, patterned relationship between baptism and the Spirit. The usual order is water baptism first followed by receiving the Spirit,

---

20. marshill.com/2011/03/21/what-does-baptism-mean-and-other-questions (July 19, 2012).

21. Hicks and Taylor, 59.

22. G. R. Beasley-Murray, *Baptism in the New Testament* (Grand Rapids, MI: Eerdmans, 1962), 80.

23. David L. Turner, *Matthew. Baker Exegetical Commentary on the New Testament* (Grand Rapids, MI: Baker, 2008), 57.

24. Robert Webber, *Ancient-Future Evangelism: Making Your Church a Faith-Forming Community* (Grand Rapids, MI: Baker, 2003), II.

25. Hicks and Taylor, 73.

but the two events occur in close proximity.[26]

In these conversion stories some physical manifestation of the Spirit indicates his arrival. Elsewhere in the New Testament the Spirit is linked most closely with energy and vitality (Lk. 24:49, Acts 1:8) and the capacity for deep personal knowing (1 Cor. 2:11-12, Rom. 8:26-27). The Spirit is always intimately connected with the word of God (1 John 2:27, John 14:26).

At what point is someone saved?

This question raises the discussion of whether in conversion salvation comes as the result of a point or a process action. In truth, it is both (1 Pet. 3:21, Acts 16:29-34).

Conversion is a process. Faith may come quickly for one person and over time and through experience to another. How are we to read the "signs of salvation" in a person's life? It takes time to reorient life habits to the new Christian ethic and worldview. In regarding salvation as a process, we see that we are "being saved" (Acts 2:42).

Yet baptism does take place at a particular moment in a person's life and in a particular place. It is the occasion on which that person is delivered over and incorporated into Christ.[27] The believer now belongs to the kingdom of the risen Christ and is no longer under the dominion of sin (Col. 1:13). On whether salvation can be had without baptism, Beasley-Murray argues the affirmative. In the same breath he quotes O.C. Quick. "We may say that, although individuals can be, and most undoubtedly are, saved without baptism, yet the world as a whole, so far as experience seems to show, could not."[28]

Is there a plan of salvation?

Hicks and Taylor describe the development of a pattern or plan for salvation in the American Restoration Movement. Alexander Campbell originally held six steps: faith, repentance, immersion, confession of sins, the gift of the Holy Spirit, and eternal life. Walter Scott put these into a "five finger exercise" for use on the Western Reserve of Ohio by dropping eternal life. T.W. Brents further refined these into what became the classic formulary: hear, believe, repent, confess, and be baptized.[29] More recently Jack Cottrell suggested the following formulation. "A sinner is saved by grace (as the basis), through faith (as the means), in baptism (as the occasion), for good works (as the result)."[30]

---

26. Ben Witherington, III, *Troubled Waters: Rethinking the Theology of Baptism* (Waco, TX: Baylor University Press, 2007), 130.

27. Arland J. Hultgren, "Baptism in the New Testament: Origins, Formulas, and Metaphors," *Word and World*, 14/1 (1994), 11.

28. O. C. Quick, *The Christian Sacraments, 2nd ed* (London: 1932), 178.

29. Hicks and Taylor, 247.

30. Jack Cottrell, "The Role of Faith in Conversion," in *Evangelicalism and the Stone-Campbell Movement*, William Baker, ed. (Downers Grove, IL: InterVarsity, 2002), 89. Quoted by Hicks and Taylor, 248.

As we saw earlier, conversion is not a simple process. To reduce the life-changing power of conversion into a simple child's formulary surely puts us onto a path where we lose both the mystery and the power of developing saving faith in Jesus.

If someone asked you, "Tell me what I would need to do to be saved?" how would you answer? Be sure to use the Bible as you formulate your response.

_____

_____

_____

_____

_____

_____

_____

_____

_____

_____

_____

Reading: Hybels, chapters 13-15

As we finish *Contagious Christian*, pay attention to Hybels' encouragement in Chapter 13 to close the sale. We are appropriately averse to using sales language when talking about sharing faith with people. Yet Hybels brings out a vital point. We often struggle to get the "ask" words out of our mouth. Those words make us tongue-tied. We feel like we are intruding into private space. That's because we are. We fear coming across wrong or putting the other person off. Or we wonder whether we have the right to be so bold as to ask someone about their salvation. Yet if John 3:16 is true and God loves people so much he was willing to die for us, isn't it worth our discomfort?

Some things are frightening to say. Here's my list of the scariest sentences.

❑ Would you like to talk about faith?

❑ Where are you in your relationship with Jesus?

❑ Would you like to explore how to become a Christian?

❑ Would you come to church with me?

What is your list of scariest sentences? Put a check by any I have given. If you have others, write them here:

_____

_____

_____

_____

_____

_____

Why do these sentences scare you?

_____

_____

_____

_____

What can you do to reduce your fear of uttering these scary sentences?

_____

_____

_____

_____

Understanding Conversion

Since conversion is such a rare and unique event in a person's life, how do we approach people who are not even considering Christianity? What do we say to those who, at the moment, are convinced that they are right where they want to be?

First, we must expect God to be involved. Without God's pursuing, seeking presence we have no reason to expect a conversion change. Since God expressed his seeking nature so clearly in Jesus we can be confident that God is out ahead of us preparing people to listen and respond to his overtures to them through us. (Remember John 3:16.)

Yet there is also a human side to this activity, both in the person who might experience conversion and in us, the ones who are prompting and encouraging the conversion process.

The Gray Matrix below helps us understand some of the challenges of conversion.[32] The vertical axis represents a knowledge scale, how much a person knows about Christianity. The horizontal axis represents a person's attitude towards

THIS WORD -COVERSION- IS SIMPLY TOO TAME AND TOO REFINED TO CAPTURE THE TRAIN WRECK THAT I EXPERIENCED . . . I KNOW OF ONLY ONE WORD TO DESCRIBE THIS . . . IMPACT.[31]

ROSARIA BUTTERFIELD

31. Rosaria Butterfield, *Secret Thoughts of an Unlikely Convert*, Kindle edition (Crown & Covenant, 2012) Loc. 83.
32. Thegraymatrix.info.

Christianity, ranging from closed to open.

Unchurched people are in the A quadrant. Their knowledge is low, they have significant misconceptions, and they have not had much if any experience with Christianity. This is where those 3G people are ("My grandparents went to church, my parents quit going, and I have never been."). People in quadrant A may never have seriously considered the claims of Jesus, but the negative faith climate created by America's defeater beliefs predisposes them to be closed towards Christianity.

The B quadrant represents people who still do not know much but their attitude has shifted from closed to open. Such a shift, often orchestrated directly by God, may be created by a change in life status, a move, a crisis that creates awareness of a need for a higher power, or the gentle influence of a committed believer. These are all influences that impact receptivity to Christianity. Once this attitude shift occurs people are not only ready to listen, they often begin to deliberately seek and ask.

Quadrant C represents people who are already Christians. They are practicing a lifestyle of faith and growing in Jesus.

People in quadrant D are the most difficult to reach, often due to a "deconversion experience." People in this quadrant typically have had a significant experience in Christianity but, for some reason, have made a conscious decision to leave their faith. They have entered the ranks of the dechurched.

The Gray Matrix

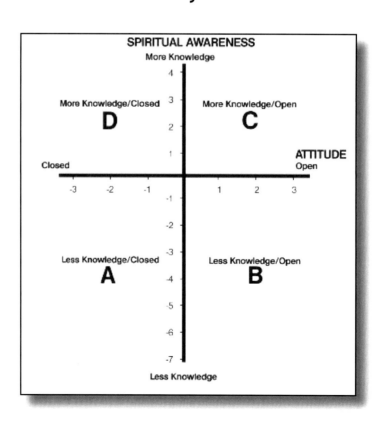

Openness and Attitude

The idea behind the Gray Matrix was first developed by James Engel and Viggo Sogaard and is commonly referred to as the Engel Scale. The Engel Scale forms the vertical knowledge axis in the Gray Matrix. At the bottom people know nothing. They progressively move up the scale as they learn more. At the 0 mark, conversion occurs and a disciple is born. As the disciple grows in faith she continues to move up the scale into the positive numbers.[33]

WHERE DO
WE BEGIN
WITH PEOPLE,
BY IMPACTING
KNOWLEDGE
OR
ADDRESSING
ATTITUDE?

As Gray used the Engel Scale in his missionary work in Southeast Asia among a largely uninterested, Buddhist people he realized that knowledge is not the only influence at work. Christianity is more than knowledge. "It (Christianity) communicates kindness, understanding, caring, patience, love and other virtues. These combine to the changing and reinforcing of attitudes among listeners while breaking down barriers towards the Gospel."[34]

Gray added the attitude axis onto the Engel Scale to capture the concept of Resistance-Receptivity described by Donald McGavran. McGavran studied movements of large numbers of people into Christian faith in India. He concluded that any group of people or individual may be placed on a Resistance-Receptivity Scale as revealed by their readiness and willingness to resist or respond positively towards the Christian message.[35] An essential evangelistic task is to look for receptivity among people so we can respond to their openness.

Engel Scale of Knowledge

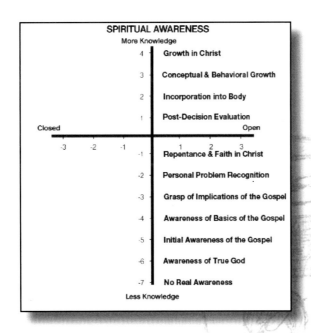

33. James F. Engle and Wilbert Norton, *What's Gone Wrong with the Harvest?* (Grand Rapids, MI: Zondervan, 1975).

34. http://thegraymatrix.info/index.php?page=14, available July 11, 2012.

35. Donald G. McGavran, *Understanding Church Growth* (Grand Rapids, MI: Zondervan, 1960), 216.

The Gray Matrix raises an important question. Where do we begin with people, by imparting knowledge or addressing attitudes?

What do you think and why?

_____

_____

_____

_____

_____

_____

Conversion Pathways

Look at the following two Gray Matrix graphs. These graphs represent the two main pathways people follow as they go through a conversion process, depending on their starting point. Unchurched people take the first pathway. If they are beginning in quadrant A (closed and less knowledgeable) they must begin by first becoming more open to exploring Christianity. As they grow more open to receiving knowledge and gaining experiential understanding, they move upward on the graph. While both knowledge and attitude are at work, we must begin by helping attitudes change before we try to do much teaching.

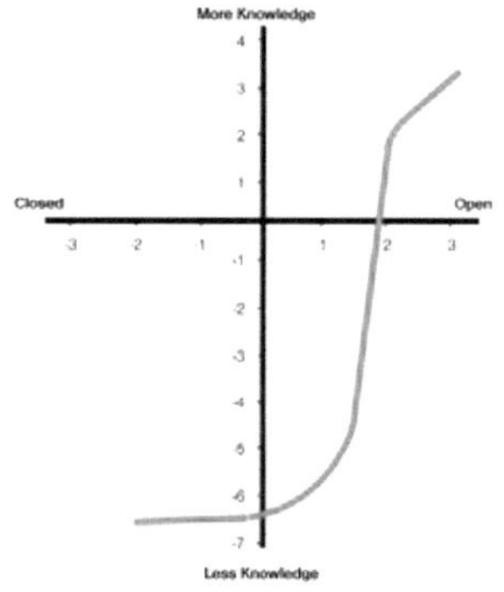

Unchurched Conversion Path 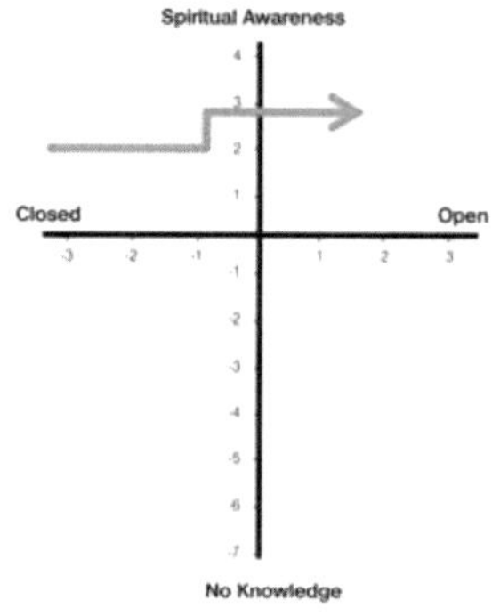   **Dechurched Conversion Path**

The second graph shows the conversion, or reconversion, process of someone in the D or dechurched quadrant. Notice this person already has significant knowledge and experience of Christianity, yet his attitude is closed. His journey towards openness will be more difficult than the unchurched person because he has been inoculated against belief. For the dechurched person an open, accepting community of believers will be critical to help work through the prejudices he has built up against Christianity and faith.

What other implications do you see in the Gray Matrix?

_____

_____

_____

How do your insights from the Gray Matrix challenge inform your understanding of how to approach people about faith in Jesus?

_____

_____

_____

_____

_____

Using A Spiritual Diagnosis Tool

In this workbook you have looked at Rainer 's U-Scale and you are practicing doing spiritual diagnoses to understand why people do not believe. Through the Gray Matrix you see how receptivity impacts the readiness of a person to hear and receive the good news of Jesus.

How can you know for sure where to plot a person on the Gray Matrix?

_____

_____

_____

_____

_____

I don't know how you answered this question, but the best way is to ask them!

Gary Rohrmayer wrote the *Your Spiritual Journey Guide*[36] as a tool to help us help people make their own spiritual diagnosis and plans. Five copies of *Your Spiritual Journey Guide* are included for you with this workbook. You can order the updated version from yourjourneyresources.com.

Your Spiritual Journey Guide is intended for use in sit down conversations. Sitting down is a talking posture. Your role is to ask a few key questions and listen, listen, listen. Remember *Your Spiritual Journey Guide* is a spiritual diagnostic and planning tool, not a Bible study.

How do you get people to sit down with you? Invite them with a question. Rohrmayer suggests you ask, "Do you believe people are on a spiritual journey?" I often ask, "Are you a believer?" Notice I don't say "Christian." That would assume too much.

These questions let people take the lead in telling you what they think and feel about spiritual life. Your response could be something like, "That is very interesting. I would love to hear more about your spiritual journey. Would you have time for me to buy you a cup of a coffee?" When you make this offer you are extending hospitality and

---

36. Gary Rohrmayer, *FirstSteps for Planting a Missional Church* (Your Journey Resources, 2006), 52-54.

showing your willingness to give to the other person by being a listener. Listening is a generous gift in our culture. Listening is not a tool to manipulate. We listen because we truly care and we want to learn what God is doing in other people's lives.

Once you get seated, thank the person for being willing to share his/her spiritual journey. This sets up the topic and shows respect. Then let the other person start. As you listen, do an internal spiritual diagnosis to determine why he or she is not a believer. (For the sake of clarity, for the rest of this discussion, I'll use refer to this person as "he," but of course it could be a woman or a man.) Ask pertinent, clarifying questions from time to time to continue showing interest. Before too much time goes by (about ten minutes) ask the first key question:

1. Where do you think Jesus fits in your spiritual journey?

Give the other person time to respond, then say something like, "Many people are interested in seeing where they are in their spiritual journey in relation to Jesus. A friend gave me this spiritual journey guide to help us do that." Pull out a copy of *Your Spiritual Journey Guide* and let him take it in his hands (this continues to give him control). You'll see very quickly if he has an interest or not. Don't push, but encourage him towards the next step with the next question. Let God do the pursuing.

2. When you look at this picture, where do you see yourself now on your spiritual journey?

Once he has had time to process the question, ask him to point out where he sees himself and to put an X at this point. This gives you both a visual marker to help make the discussion more real.

3. Where would you like to be on your spiritual journey in six months to a year?

We believe that God is pursuing people, calling them towards himself. Because you're talking about a spiritual journey there is a natural inclination to movement. When you ask this question you are inviting the other person to grow, to deliberately think about and plan to go on this spiritual journey. Invite him to make a second X at the point he would like to be in 6 months to a year.

4. What is standing between you and that point?

This question helps him identify barriers against faith in his life. This is where he will reveal his reasons for not believing. His answers will confirm or adjust the spiritual diagnosis you have done in your head.

5. What will it take for you to remove those barriers?

Now you are giving him the opportunity to make a plan. The point of this question is not to give you the chance to share the gospel with him at this time; it is to help him recognize faith barriers while building the expectation that his current situation can change. You are helping him

A SPIRITUAL DIAGNOSIS HELPS A PERSON PLAN A PATH TOWARD FAITH

develop his own personalized plan for spiritual discovery.

6. How could I help you on your spiritual journey?

This is your final question. You are continuing to extend your hospitality as a spiritual guide. You also provide the opportunity to think about next steps. At this point he may need you to introduce him to more resources. Typical resources could be a readable modern translation of the Bible (often non-Christians have a King James Version as the only Bible available to them), an invitation to a missional community, a small group or a party, or the opportunity to meet again.

This entire conversation can typically occur in about thirty minutes. Keep it moving forward. Be aware of the time so you do not overextend his interest or time availability. Finally, always leave the conversation with the open invitation for the next step.

When time is up, sincerely thank him for sharing his spiritual journey with you, his barriers to faith, and his ideas on next steps. If he seems unwilling to commit to a next step at that time, ask his permission to send him information on events and opportunities that your church is doing.[37] If you don't already have his contact information, get it now. Be sure to pass it on to whoever keeps up the database at your church with a note that this person is a Jesus seeker.

Action Step

You need to begin practicing using *Your Spiritual Journey Guide* on a regular basis. You will feel awkward at first. You may feel embarrassed and you will certainly feel hesitant. I've known people to break out in cold, shaking sweats in their car thinking about having this conversation with the person they are meeting. Push through these feelings. Remember, Jesus loves people far more than you will ever be able to. He died for them. All you have to do is be interested in their stories and ask these few questions.

Reporting

Your goal is to have five sit-down conversations in which you use *Your Spiritual Journey Guide*. Keep track of these conversations under lesson 7 of your Personal Answer Book.

---

37. Scott Christensen, lead planter of the Renovo: A Church of Christ in Puyallup, Washington calls this ongoing connection "drip irrigation." By drip irrigating regularly you keep Jesus and your church at the forefront of a person's mind.

Unit D
Connecting With God's Lost People

It is part of the nature and character of God to seek his people. The idea of God as trinity—God the Father, God the Son, and God the Holy Spirit—is relationship. A God who has relationships at the core of his being is a God who seeks to connect. In this section we'll look at ways we can connect with people who do not yet believe and so are, in Bible terms, lost.

Deborah's Conversion

The following story comes from Ron and Lori Clark, church planters at the Agape Church of Christ in downtown Portland, Oregon.

Deborah was a witch/psychic. She had connected with some of our Dignity Village (a homeless community) crew and told Lori that she was in an abusive relationship.

She came to our worship service on Halloween morning 2011 with bruising around one of her eyes. She was planning to be critical of the sermon that day, "What Do We Do With Harry Potter?" She had taught the Satanic Bible in a group she joined after she left the Jehovah's Witnesses. She was very critical of Christianity and what we were about. However, she felt safe and loved by her friends who are part of our church and her initial contacts with Lori for help.

In the sermon I shared that I had studied with a Satanist in the past and how he had been mistreated by Christian kids when he was young. He clung to Satanism because it expresses a sense of choice, morality, and group support. I read the "10 points of Satanism" from Anton LaVey's Book of Satan. I saw Deborah mouthing the sentences like she had memorized them. My main point was that Satanism, witchcraft, Harry Potter, or magic are not something to be feared. This philosophy gives us opportunity to show Christ's power, love, and justice to people who are hurting and disillusioned with a movement that is supposed to demonstrate love and mercy.

Deborah thanked me afterward and said she felt very safe here. She also appreciated the honest way we dealt with the Biblical texts as well as other "religious groups."

She kept coming to Agape. Our praise team invited Deborah to their practices and one Sunday she sang with the group. She joined our home community for Thanksgiving and opened up about her fears and need for safe relationships.

Deborah was baptized during our Christmas service in 2011. On New Year's Day 2012 the INS picked her up not following appropriate protocols when she entered the US from Scotland. Deborah was sent to a detention facility in Tacoma for immigration violators.

We contacted a lawyer who handled the cases at the detention facility. He told us he enjoyed visiting Deborah. She was ready to go back to England but missed her church. He said, "She is doing well. The others in the jail tell us that she is always singing and is teaching the women at chapel on Sundays a lot of new songs she learned in Portland." It is amazing how being included for a short time in a church and a chance to sing with others impacted her life in a dark time.

Deborah is back in England now. She is struggling to find a church. We can only pray for her now and stay in touch on Facebook. However, we know that God has touched a life that may not have been touched if we had not started Agape.

Lesson 8:
Servant Evangelism

People are pretty skeptical. We hear about people getting ripped off all the time. It has probably happened to you. That makes it hard to trust. On the flip side, people today like to serve others. Volunteerism in America is strong. In 2010, 62.8 million adults volunteered over 8 billion hours in local and national organizations.[1] If we are to connect authentically with people we are going to have to walk our walk as Christians.

The Great Commission

Luke 24:45-48 The Resurrection

Then he opened their minds to understand the Scriptures. And he said, "Yes, it was written long ago that the Messiah would suffer and die and rise from the dead on the third day. It was also written that this message would be proclaimed in the authority of his name to all the nations, beginning in Jerusalem: 'There is forgiveness of sins for all who repent.' You are witnesses of all these things."

There they were, the eleven remaining apostles and the two men from Emmaus, barricaded in a room, filled with dismay and fright, struggling to understand how Jesus' life and their dreams had ended so badly. Then, suddenly, Jesus was there, asking them, *"Why are you afraid! Why can't you believe? Touch my hands. Look at my feet. I am not a ghost. I am real"* (Luke 24:38-40).

It is this same unbelief that people struggle with today. We can explain how someone who is deathly ill, in a coma, or even resuscitated can recover and return to active life. But for the dead, the truly dead—the three days past dead—to rise to walk and talk and dress and eat again, is beyond belief.

Luke's Great Commission account places Jesus' resurrection firmly and historically at the core of the message that was to be proclaimed. We can become so engrossed in arguments, in acts of humanitarian service, or in treading carefully around the landmines of political correctness that we can forget that the central message of our faith was first stated by an angel: *"He isn't here! He's risen from the dead"* (Luke 24:6)!

Any time we share faith we eventually must get down to this bare earth question, "Do you believe Jesus rose from the dead or not?" This is a pretty in-your-face question. It doesn't leave wiggle room. One either does or doesn't believe in Jesus' resurrection.

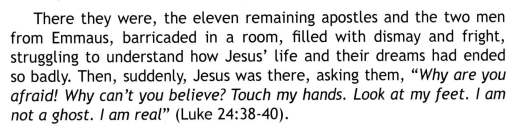

---

1. volunteeringinamerica.gov, July 14, 2012.

Arguments for the Resurrection

Surprised by Hope is N.T. Wright's marvelous attempt to argue the reality of the resurrection to our skeptical world. The following is a summary of Wright's essential arguments for the resurrection.

It is incredibly hard to believe Jesus rose from the dead. There must be another explanation. Here are other choices, with a response to each.

1. Jesus didn't really die. He was drugged and revived in the tomb (Matthew 27:47).

Answer: Roman soldiers knew how to kill people.

2. When the women went to the tomb, they saw someone and mistook him for Jesus (Matthew 28:1-10).

Answer: They would have figured it out soon enough when Jesus didn't show up again.

3. Jesus only appeared to people who believed in him (1 Corinthians 15:1-9).

Answer: Neither Thomas (John 20:24-29) nor Paul (Acts 9:1-6) believed until they saw Jesus alive.

4. These biblical accounts are biased.

Answer: So what's new? History and journalism are biased too.

5. The disciples began by saying, "He will be raised," which changed over time to, "He has been raised." The two are functionally equivalent.

Answer: No, they're not.

6. Lots of people have visions of loved ones appearing to them.

Answer: The disciples' first reaction was that Jesus was a ghost (Luke 24:37), but ghosts don't have bodies (Luke 24:39).

7. The disciples had a wonderfully rich spiritual experience. (Wright says this is the most popular explanation.)[2]

Answer: "Resurrection was and is the defeat of death, not simply a nicer description of it ..."

Why did Christianity grow like wildfire? Rodney Stark estimates that by 350 A.D. Christians numbered more than thirty-three million, over half of the population of the Roman Empire.[3] Wright argues that the heart of the growth of Christianity lies in the fact that the resurrection was a true historical event.

Why should we accept the resurrection as true? The answer lies in two facts and three observations.

---

2. N. T. Wright, *Surprised by Hope* (New York: Harper One, 2008), 61-62.

3. Rodney Stark, *The Rise of Christianity* (Princeton: Princeton University Press, 1996), 7.

Two Facts

1. The tomb was empty.

2. Witnesses saw Jesus alive.

Three Observations

1. The disciples were hardly likely to suffer and die as they did for a lie.

2. The early church emphasized the first day of the week as their special day for worship; they called this day the Lord's Day. Such dedication to a day is difficult to understand unless something utterly memorable happened on that day.

3. What power could affect such radical change in so many people's lives, across such an expanse of human history, unless that power was alive?

At face value these two brief facts and three small statements hardly seem able to support the most central of our faith assertions. Yet it is their simple witness to truth that makes them powerful. Michael Green sums up these ideas, saying, "the power these Christians had to love each other, to overcome character defects, to endure opposition and death gladly for the sake of Jesus" was one of the central appeals for Christian belief.[4]

Reading: Poole, Introduction through Chapter 2

Garry Poole's *Seeker Small Groups* will be our guide towards the final strategic assignment of *Sharing Faith*. Take a few moments at this point to turn to the Strategic Assignment section of this workbook, beginning on page 101. Look over the assignment. From this point on your activities will build towards your strategic assignment of conducting a seeker small group.

Poole includes many stories of people as they moved along their journey of becoming Christians. As you read these stories do two things. First, identify where each person began on Rainer's U-Scale. Second, practice doing a spiritual diagnosis and see if you can identify which of the four main reasons explain why each of them was not a Christian. Write your observations in the margin of your book as you read.

In these first chapters Poole helps us see that being part of a group helps people become Christians. In fact, our experience is that people catch faith better when they are exploring Christianity with others who are not yet believers either. This is a critical insight. People like to become Christians with others who are also becoming Christians.

---

4. Michael Green, *Evangelism in the Early Church* (Grand Rapids, MI: Eerdmans, 1970, 2003), 159.

Characteristics of a Seeker Group

What is a seeker group?

PEOPLE LIKE
TO BECOME
CHRISTIANS
WITH
OTHERS WHO
ARE BECOMING
CHRISTIANS.

1. The purpose of a seeker group is to provide pre- or post-Christian seekers the opportunity to explore Christianity and consider faith together. This purpose will guide what is done in a seeker group.

2. A seeker group is small enough so people can build relationships with one another. Poole suggests between two and twelve people. Yet the Alpha course (we'll talk more about Alpha later) may have hundreds of people in the same course. What Alpha does is to gather people into table-sized groups for talking. In a home, you can have ten, twenty, or thirty people who sub-divide into smaller table groups to talk. Here's your rule of thumb: a seeker group can include as many as can comfortably sit around a table and talk—but you can use multiple tables!

3. The non-Christians (when they accept your invitation to a group they become seekers) outnumber the Christians. This is critical. If there are more Christians than seekers you have a Bible study, not a seeker group.

4. A seeker group is a safe place to explore life. Notice I do not say "spiritual life." Why? Because most seekers are concerned about daily life, not spiritual conversations. Being in a safe place means:

- They can reveal themselves without fear.

- No question is off limits.

- They are allowed to discover spiritual truths on their own, not through a sermon that they cannot challenge.

Which of the above characteristics caught your attention most and why?

_____

_____

_____

_____

_____

_____

_____

_____

_____

_____

Think about groups you have been part of. Were any of them seeker groups? Why or why not?

_____

_____

_____

_____

_____

_____

What is Servant Evangelism?

The concept of servant evangelism has been around for a long time. The people of Israel were commanded to care for strangers among them because they were once strangers (Exodus 22:21). Jesus, in the Golden Rule, said, *"Do to others whatever you would like them to do to you"* (Matthew 7:12). The prophet Isaiah spoke of the suffering servant in chapter 53. Jesus said, *"For I was hungry, and you fed me. I was thirsty, and you gave me a drink. I was a stranger, and you invited me into your home."* These verses are all expressions of a witness to the love and compassion of God through the kindness his people show to others.

The term "servant evangelism" was coined in 1985 by Steve Sjogren, founding pastor of Vineyard Community Church in Cincinnati, Ohio, which grew from thirty-seven people to over six thousand over the course of a decade. In his book *Conspiracy of Kindness* Sjogren defines servant evangelism as "demonstrating the kindness of God by offering to do some acts of humble service with no strings attached."[5] His premise is that if we are willing to participate in acts of love and kindness to those outside our circle through humble acts of service, God's love will plant a seed that has the chance to blossom into faith.

Servant evangelism is part of a constellation of ideas that runs from acts of kindness at its simplest, to service as an expression of values, to social justice as a theological mandate. We can picture this in the diagram below where random acts of kindness by individuals anchor the left side of the horizontal scale and organized, political activities anchor the right. The vertical scale shows intended impact with low at the bottom and high at the top. Servant evangelism falls approximately within the shaded area.

Servant evangelism can be done in so many ways—by passing out quarters at laundromats, offering free car washes, conducting light bulb and soda giveaways, even cleaning toilets.

---

5. Steve Sjogren, *Conspiracy of Kindness*, rev. ed. (Ventura: Regal, 2008), 18.

You can download Sjogren's list of ninety-four servant evangelism ideas at http://bit.ly/1IHuQ3X.

Kind actions, however, do not themselves constitute evangelism. What makes acts of kindness different from service evangelism is the verbal communication of the gospel.

This puts us in a bit of an emotional bind. It's easy to go around doing good, and many people will want to join us. But when we say something about Jesus it feels like we're pulling a bait and switch tactic, as if we're saying, "I'll do something good for you if you'll let me tell you

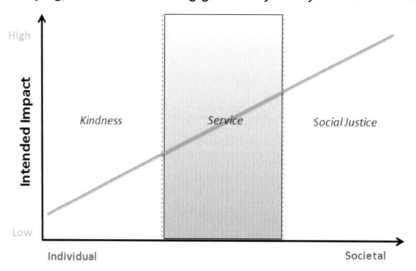

about Jesus."

How, then, should we approach servant evangelism?

First, let's talk about kindness. You've heard of "random acts of kindness," in which we're encouraged to do something kind for someone, like purchasing a latte for the next customer at Starbucks. Christians are supposed to be people who are living representatives of God, Jesus, and the Holy Spirit. One characteristic of the Godhead is kindness. In Psalm 136 David repeats the phrase *"His loving kindness endures forever"* over and over again. We should practice kindness because it's who we are. It's our nature to do good. Doing good is a by-product of our new life in Jesus. I love what Steve Sjogren says: "I have become kind of hooked on showing people generosity, kindness, and respect whenever I get the chance."[6]

Service occurs when we become more deliberate about our acts of kindness. We set out to help people with a goal in mind. Examples of service might be giving people a good meal, building people homes, supplying children with school supplies. Acts of service are what we do because we are compassionate, caring people like our father in heaven and we believe the world should be a better place.

Kindness and service become evangelism only when we deliberately attach a message about faith to our actions. Confessions of faith don't

---

6. Steve Sjogren, servantevangelism.com/articles/why-serve-flows-from-me, November 4, 2011.

have to be huge. They can be something simple like the name and website of your church on the water bottle label, a sign that says, "Provided by Lighthouse Church," or a contact card printed with your web address and "Call us when we can serve you next."[7]

What is the purpose of servant evangelism? First, servant evangelism works against the defeater beliefs of American society. The mayor of New Brunswick, New Jersey, says of the Brunswick Church of Christ, "When we think of a church that helps our community, we think of you." The work the church does in that town can serve to soften the attitudes of unbelievers they meet. Second, practicing servant evangelism as a church enables the congregation to engage their community on the community's terms. It gets us outside our meeting places to meet people, deliberately and with purpose, face to face. Renovo church in Puyallup, WA runs a face-painting booth with free helium balloons at every Farmers' Market. While they're working, they offer people the opportunity to complete a contact card to receive information from Renovo.

Finally, servant evangelism sows good seeds. Servant evangelism does not typically change the lives of unchurched people, bring them into our worship services, or grow our churches.[8] It does, however, bring more goodness into the world and it keep the church focused outwardly. And, if we keep sowing seeds, at some point we can expect good fruit.

Three Steps to Servant Evangelism Impact

How do we maximize the faith impact of servant evangelism? By using this three-step approach.

Step 1: Do THEIR things in THEIR places.

Instead of inviting people into what your church is doing, serve in the community in an event that is already taking place. Help with their ideas (their things) under their organization (their places). But how do you plug into these community events? Start by taking an inventory of what is happening in your neighborhood or community. Find out what events are taking place in area schools. Find out what local service agencies and your local chamber of commerce are doing. Go to their events and join in. As a guest in their space, you should be circumspect about what you say about your faith. In their space, play by their rules. This shows respect and builds trust.

Step 2: Do THEIR things in OUR places.

At this step, do some of the same things that are already happening (their things) but take on the organization (our places) to extend that

7. Steve Sjogren, servantevangelism.com/articles/why-i-use-outreach-connect-cards-and-think-you-should-too/#.UDP7UkR9n54, August 10, 2012.

8. Chris Eldrod, "Servant Evangelism Myths," pastorelrod.wordpress.com/2008/02/11/servant-evangelism-myths/, February 11, 2008.

service into new areas, communities, or to new people. Become the organizing force. This is what makes it "our places." By "places" I'm not talking about geographic place but ownership. As you organize, invite non-Christians to serve with you. If they join you, accept the fact that they have voluntarily stepped over a line. They have entered into our spaces where we have much more opportunity to speak about why we are doing this service ... because of Jesus.

Step 3: Do OUR things in OUR places.

In this case, both the idea and the ownership are ours. Again, we invite non-Christians to join us in these activities, but here we are overtly Christian. They will expect to join into devotionals, prayer times, and such because they know they are in our space. When people step into "our things in our places," we should be confident in asking them about their spiritual lives. They have, by joining us, given us implicit permission to share faith with them.

Invite your non-Christian friends and neighbors to serve with you. Make them part of your team. If they join you they have made a decision to accept your offer and be part of God's things.

Action Step

This week I want you to practice one more way of engaging people in spiritual conversations. I learned this while taking my students from Cascade College onto the light rail train in Portland. We would sit or stand next to strangers and strike up faith conversations. It was scary—and amazing!

Start with the easiest person on your list (from week 5 of your Personal Answer Book) and invite him to join you somewhere you can sit and talk. Take him out to lunch; buy her a Starbucks. Tell him you've been thinking a lot about God and faith and that you'd like his insight. There is an important question for you to ask, but first, there are two important rules to follow.

Rule 1: Don't wait around and talk about everything else first then bring up this question when you're running out of time.

You've asked your friend out for a reason. Sit down, get situated, then ask your question.

Rule 2: Don't ask what he thinks. Ask him what others think.

There's something about working in the third person that frees people up to talk. They'll end up telling you what they think anyway, but you're asking them about others.

Ready? Here's the question:

I've been doing a lot of thinking lately about why some people believe in God and others don't. It's a really complex subject. What do people you know—people at work, friends, family—think about God?

Don't ask the question unless you really have been thinking about this lately which, since you're working on this module, I assume you have. While they're talking, listen carefully for anything that sounds like a defeater belief. I'm confident you can recognize those beliefs by now. When you think you've heard one, practice your reflective listening skills and say it back to them as clearly, accurately, and as strongly as you can.

Don't feel like you have to keep digging around. Have a comfortable time together. Enjoy the time with a friend. When you feel it's appropriate, thank him for his insights and tell him how helpful his thoughts have been. Then get on with your day.

Recording

Turn to lesson 8 in your Personal Answer Book and begin recording your experiences.

Missional Director Meeting

Sit down with your missional director for Meeting #3.

Lesson 9: Extending Invitations

Joe's Journey

I have been studying with Joe-the-ex-Mormon every Wednesday morning for over two years now, which is about how long it takes me to get through the Book of Luke with someone if we meet once a week.

Joe attends our worship services more faithfully than some Christians. He helps load the trailer every week after worship and partners with his wife in running our Financial Peace University ministry. He feels good about being here because, as he says, "Wilson, you explain things from the Bible better than anyone who has ever tried to teach me."

Mario also showed up this particular morning. Mario is one seriously Godly Guatamalan who does an honest day's (or night's) work driving freight for Safeway. So he does not come every week, since usually he has worked all night. But he was present this morning—by the providence of God.

When we finished the passage where Jesus says, "Why do doubts arise in your minds?" it was time to put a wee bit o' pressure on ol' Joe.

"Joe, you know God is pursuing you, don't you?"

He smiled and nodded.

I spoke of all God has done to keep him connected, and to put us in each other's lives. He smiled and nodded again.

"Joe, one of three things is going to happen here: One, You are going to let God pursue you your whole life and never surrender (not likely). Two, You are going to needlessly wait longer to surrender when you know it is inevitable. Or, three, You can just surrender right now."

Joe raised his eyebrows and pursed his lips.

I then told Joe a story I watched recently on the Weather Channel. An older guy was kayaking for the first time with his son on a dam-fed river. Too much water was released and he was stranded, holding on to a low-hanging branch, about to be swept away. The Coast Guard was called. A rescuer was lowered on a cable. He successfully attached a harness around the kayaker and was about to lift him to safety, but ...

The kayaker wouldn't let go of the expensive, rented kayak.

The rescuer finally convinced the kayaker to let go and up they went into the helicopter. Only from the perspective of the helicopter did he fully see the danger he had been in.

Mario, who speaks English as second language, then said, "AHH, so the guy from helicopter was a-coming down, and the other guy wouldn't let go of the kayak—So, Joe, what kayak you holdin' on to?"

I got up to leave. The two of them were going to stay a while longer.

I simply said, "Joe, Let go of the kayak, man."

Reading: Poole, Chapters 3-4

The heart of Poole's book is chapters 3-8. These chapters cover how to invite people to a seeker group, what to do during a seeker group, and tips and tools to be a group leader.

In chapter 3 Poole discusses extending irresistible invitations. By this time you shouldn't feel nearly as intimidated by asking people to attend a seeker group because you've been doing a lot of talking with people who are unchurched or dechurched. Hopefully you have developed several significant relationships with people and had spiritual conversation with many of them.

Portions of this chapter may have brought these new conversations to mind.

Look over Poole's list of seekers' fears on pages 81-84. Think about two people with whom you have had spiritual conversations during this study. What fears could you anticipate them having about an invitation from you?

Person:

_____

Fears:

_____

_____

_____

_____

_____

Person:

_____

Fears:

_____

_____

_____

_____

How do these fears compare to those shared in Laura Atchley's story on p. 96 of Poole's book?

_____

_____

_____

_____

_____

Now look over the invitation guidelines on Poole, pages 84-90. Pay particular attention to #8—Ask for a Yes or No Response. Write out an invitation you could use with one of the people above:

_____

_____

_____

_____

_____

_____

_____

_____

We're getting a bit ahead of ourselves now, but this is a great time to begin thinking about what you will do in the future. After reading chapter 4 on first meetings, write out the seven pieces of a seeker group meeting below. Feel free to refer to Appendix A to remind you how these pieces go together.

1.　**The Setting**

2.　_____

3.　_____

4.　_____

5.　_____

6.　_____

7.　**Conclusion**

Your Strategic Assignment

"Your assignment should you choose to accept it ...;" that's the way every Mission Impossible movie begins. Once you read about your strategic assignment you may feel like Ethan Hunt. But you can do it!

Your strategic assignment for this module is to form a team of four other Christians, train them to become evangelistic bringers, and together start a seeker group where at least fifty percent of the people are either unchurched or dechurched. Your goal is to lead a team who learn how to be evangelistic bringers and to run a seeker group.

If you're married, you and your spouse will ask two other couples to join you to invite enough people so that at least three unchurched or dechurched couples will join you in this short-term seeker group.

Do these have to be couples? Does everyone have to be married? No, of course not. But if you're married it's most likely the people you will invite will also be married.

From this point forward we'll work on accomplishing this seeker group together. Garry Poole's book *Seeker Small Groups* will be a guide to help you.

Seeker Small Groups is a great resource for you, but it is asking a lot at this point to have you prepare the material for every small group meeting. For this strategy assignment you will use the Sycamore Series #1, *The Life* material produced by Let's Start Talking. This study contains five units on Jesus' life. Garry Poole chose the Sycamore Series as the top small group evangelism tool for 2010.[9]

Action Step

Order the Sycamore Training DVD ($19.99) and two packs of Sycamore Series # 1, *The Life* ($25 each) from friendspeak.org.

Recruiting Your Team

It's time to recruit your team. You're looking for two other couples, or four individuals, who will commit to starting and running a seeker group with you. Your biggest challenge will be to help your team become evangelistic bringers. Everything else is fairly straightforward.

The first step in recruiting your team is to have your expectations clearly in mind. Here's what you're asking your team to do:

1. Commit to eight weeks of gatherings. Three weeks will be for training and inviting, and five for the seeker group itself.

2. Pray over guests whom the group will invite.

3. Invite people to attend.

4. Be good table leaders and helpers during the seeker group.

This is a short list. It is memorable and specific. Let me break it down even further for you.

Eight Weeks of Gatherings

Your seeker group will run five consecutive weeks. Prior to that you want to train your team, practice, and become familiar with the material. Each of these training meetings will run two hours. Below is an outline of the eight weeks, so you can clearly describe the meetings to the team members you are inviting to join you.

9. February 2, 2010, outreachmagazine.com/resources/3423-Outreach-Magazine-Announces-7th-Annual-Outreach-Resources-the-Year.

Week 1—Overview

During overview week you will introduce your team to the Sycamore Series material. You will assemble your list of people to pray for and invite and begin your prayers for them.

Week 2—Training

Your team will watch and talk through the Sycamore Training DVD to learn how to be table leaders and helpers for a seeker group. You will also begin making your invitations.

Week 3—Model Evening

You will run your team through the first unit doing everything just like you will for all five seeker group weeks. This will provide you a practice run and the opportunity to iron out kinks before they happen.

Prayer is your constant resource to release God's divine attention. Not only will you train your team to be evangelistic bringers, table leaders and helpers, you will also train them for specific, purposeful prayer.

You and your team will create an invitation list, just like you would to throw a party. (In fact, that's really what you'll be doing with a seeker group. Jesus will be the guest of honor.) Your invitation list will also be the prayer list for your team.

Invite Your Guests

Inviting may be the most critical activity in this process. Once you develop your invitation list and pray for specific people, you will invite them to your group. You can't, and shouldn't, do this alone. In fact, one sign of a good leader is the ability to help others learn and grow. You will train your team members to become evangelistic bringers, people who will invite and bring people they know to the seeker group.[10] You now have a number of tools at your disposal to help them do this, such as: praying for waitstaff, the 3 questions, 3-step conversations, and conducting spiritual diagnoses. Now that you are practicing these activities, you can train your team to do them too.

Be Table Leaders and Helpers

During the Sycamore Series group meetings you and your team will act as table leaders and helpers. We'll talk more about this work later. At first, all you need to tell them is that table leaders and helpers create a welcoming atmosphere where your guests feel free to ask honest questions about faith and Jesus.

As you meet these first three weeks, talk about your invitation experiences. Keep praying for people. Share light refreshments together.

---

10. Tim Keller, *Redeemer Church Planting Manual* (New York: Redeemer Church Planting Center, 2002), 119.

Action Step:

Assemble Your team.

Who are you thinking of? Who are the people God is whispering about for you to include on your team? Don't assume your best friends will jump on board with you. They may be the first to tell you no. If they do refuse, don't be upset. Thank them and say something like, "Maybe next time. Could I keep you informed about what we see God doing during this group?"

Recording

Turn to lesson 9 in your Personal Answer Book and begin your team assembly.

Unit E
Creating Seeker Groups

Lauren Winner[1] did not come to Jesus all at once. In her memoir, *Girl Meets God*, Winner says she didn't have the archetypical conversion story—no Road to Damascus epiphany, no date she can point to and say, "That's the day I became a Christian."

The decision to raise Lauren and her sister Jewish was made by her Reform Jewish father and her Southern Baptist mother before they married. She grew up celebrating Passover and Rosh Hashanah, and attending a Sunday School at the local temple. In her teens, Winner not only embraced her Jewishness, but looked for ways to pursue it deeper, eventually choosing the difficult path of becoming an Orthodox Jew.

Lauren Winner

The more Winner studied the Torah, observed Sabbath and kosher laws and other Jewish rituals, the more she found herself drawn to Christianity. She was impressed but not convinced by the idea of the incarnation, that God could be at once transcendent and present. The convincing came to her in a dream. When she awoke, she knew "about the reality of Jesus. The truth of Him. That He was a person whose pronouns you had to capitalize. That He was God."[2]

She went to her Rabbi, then to her boyfriend, and finally to her high school physics teacher, the only practicing Christian she knew. She signed up for a class on Christianity at a nearby church. The class frustrated and enraged her, made her question why so many Christians are running away from Christ. Putting words to the frustration, though, made her realize she was doing the same thing—running from Christ.

She decided to be baptized, but not yet. She gave herself another two years to find a church, study more, build herself a community of faith.

Community was important to Lauren, as it is to most people who embark on a journey of faith. She valued her relationships with the people who walked with her through her early days of Christianity. They were the ones who knew her when. The people in the church in Oxford where she was baptized were not the sort of people she would have been naturally drawn to. But they held a piece of her story as she sought Jesus and was sought by him. Their lives had become a part of her own.

---

1. Photo Source: laurenwinner.com
2. Lauren Winner, *Girl Meets God*. (New York: Random House, 2002), 51, 56.

Lesson 10
Coming to Faith in Community

People like to come to faith with others who are doing the same. Your strategic assignment, to conduct a seeker group, allows this to happen.

Your first step in developing a community was to gather your team. How is it going? Have you asked the people on your list yet?

In this section we'll look at conversion patterns and walk through, in some detail, what you'll do in the seeker group meeting.

The Great Commission

John 20:21-23 One God

The Gospel of John is my favorite evangelistic book in the Bible. John is full of stories of people who meet Jesus—religious leaders, foreign soldiers, followers of other religions, and people in complete humiliation. Each encounter reveals Jesus in a new way as each person tries to understand him in the context of his or her life. At its heart, that's what a seeker group should be, the place where people meet Jesus and try to understand who he is.

Again he said, "Peace be with you. As the Father has sent me, so I am sending you." Then he breathed on them and said, "Receive the Holy Spirit. If you forgive anyone's sins, they are forgiven. If you do not forgive them, they are not forgiven."

John's commissioning scene is spare in action but full in implication. That Sunday evening, as the disciples huddled in fear behind locked doors, Jesus entered into their hiding place, expelled their fear with peace, and commissioned them to be the messengers of kingdom. This was the risen Lord Jesus at work, in the flesh.

Exploring "One" God

Let's begin this exploration into the exclusivity of Jesus with the biblical context. In the world of the Old Testament, and even the New Testament, belief in a plurality of deities and powers was the norm. We see this in the Bible in places like Exodus 20:3, which says, *"You must not have any other god but me,"* and Acts 17:16 which reads, *"While Paul was waiting for them in Athens, he was deeply troubled by all the idols he saw everywhere in the city."* Yet in the midst of this polytheistic world, God revealed himself as the one God, creator, sustainer, and the ultimate source of life and goodness.

The Israelite belief in this one God YHWH (Jehovah) was grounded in their irreducible confession of faith, the Shema (Deut. 6:4). "Hear O Israel, the Lord your God, the Lord is one." The first of the Ten Commandments (Ex. 20:2-6; Deut. 5:6-10) called for Israel's allegiance to YHWH above any other god, power, or ruling force. "Everywhere in the Hebrew Scriptures, it is this one God who manifests his character and acts in human history both redemptively and in terms of revelation... The Israelites viewed God as unique and thus uniquely worthy of worship."[3]

In this theocentric, monotheistic worldview of Israel, YHWH also claimed his right as the universal God "to whom all nations, kings, and even emperors must finally submit."[4] This is the context of the gospel of John in which Jesus claimed the identity of YHWH. Translated into the Greek world, Jesus was *kyrios Christos* (Christ the Lord) which became the ultimate confession of Christian belief through the phrase "Jesus is Lord," *kyrios Iesous* (Acts 2:36; Rom. 10:9; 1 Cor. 12:3; Phil 2:11). These were powerful words. A person lived or died, spiritually and sometimes physically, by their willingness to confess or deny Jesus as Lord.

> O LORD, YOU ARE OUR FATHER. WE ARE THE CLAY, YOU ARE THE POTTER; WE ARE ALL THE WORK OF YOUR HAND.
>
> ISAIAH 64:8

From its inception the early church claimed the throne of divinity for the Lord Jesus. (Acts 2:14-41) Bauckman says,"The highest possible Christology, the inclusion of Jesus in the unique divine identity, was central to the faith of the early church even before any of the New Testament writings were written."[5] John used this conceptualization of Jesus as deity as the foundation for the seven "I am" statements of Jesus that appropriate the divine designation "I AM." The story of Jesus is thus the story of God's personal mission to deliver people from sin.

With Jesus firmly included in the identity of God, God is conceived in relational terms. Here is the power of the Trinitarian conception. The one God of the Shema is known in completeness only through his self-revelation as God the Father, God the Son, and God the Holy Spirit—the three in one God.

As the physical manifestation of God, Jesus is the authorized emissary who speaks on God's behalf in this commissioning scene of John. Jesus represents God's redemptive mission under which the Father-Son relationship exists. It is the Father who sends the Son, and the Father and the Son who send the Spirit.

As the leader of this divine salvation mission, Jesus inaugurates the messianic age in which he will gather God's children into one community (John 11:52), indwelt by the Father, Son, and Holy Spirit, and "formed into a community whose love is a magnetic force to a watching world (John 13:35; 17:20-23)."[6] Thus the mission in which the Lord Jesus leads

3. Andreas J. Kostenberger, *A Theology of John's Gospel and Letters* (Grand Rapids, MI: Zondervan, 2009), 356-357.

4. Christopher J.H. Wright, *The Mission of God: Unlocking the Bible's Grand Narrative* (Downers Grove, IL: InterVarsity Press, 2006), 105.

5. Richard Bauckham, *God Crucified: Monotheism and Christology in the New Testament* (Grand Rapids, MI: Eerdmans, 1998), 27.

6. Kostenberger, *A Theology of John's Gospel and Letters*, 541.

his disciples is rooted in the unity of the Father, Son, and Spirit and mimics their pattern of obedience. As the Son obeys the Father, so the disciples obey the Son. To do otherwise is to fall back into the rebellion that followed creation.

How do you relate your confession of Jesus as Lord with your obedience to him?

_____

_____

_____

_____

_____

_____

_____

_____

_____

_____

_____

Reading: Poole, Chapters 5-7

In these three chapters Poole touches on the essentials of a seeker group: asking questions, listening, and developing your unit plan.

Ask Great Questions

If having more seekers than Christians is the defining characteristic of a seeker group, asking questions is the essential process. Your goal is not to be the teacher, the expert who gives information. The Bible and the Sycamore Series will fill the role of information giver for you. Your goal is to help people ask the questions they might not ask otherwise, and to provide a safe context for their questions. As Poole says, "Most seekers have never fully considered what they believe or why they believe it."[7]

Poole's book gives you good information about how to form questions, yet we need to simplify the process even more than he does. Our goal is to learn a simple way to run a seeker group that provides a powerful means to help people explore faith. Some of the key things we can do to accomplish this deal with what question we ask and how.

The best groups often only use two questions. These questions, which I learned from the Alpha Course, have become my staples.

1. What do you think about this?

2. How do you feel about this?

7. Poole, 121.

The first question, "What do you think?" draws people's attention to the facts and realities. During the "thinking" discussion, keep asking questions to help people dig deeper. You can use Poole's questions on observation and interpretation for this.

What is the purpose of observation questions?

_____

_____

_____

_____

What do interpretation questions do?

_____

_____

_____

You'll find people take about fifteen to twenty minutes to work through the thinking question. Allow the discussion on the thinking question to die down, then move on to the feeling question. The feeling question helps people comprehend implications and their responses. Poole's reflection and application questions come into play at this point.

What do reflection questions do?

_____

_____

_____

_____

Why are application questions helpful in determining how someone feels?

_____

_____

_____

_____

Poole defines an icebreaker as a nonthreatening question that everyone can feel comfortable answering. What function does an icebreaker perform?

_____

_____

Icebreakers are important, but it's tough to find good ones. Another trick I learned from Alpha is to use a joke or a funny story in place of an icebreaker. I can't tell you exactly why it works, but a good joke warms up the room and gets people in the mood for the discussion.

Listen Well

Poole says, "We want to give our seeking friends an opportunity to identify their toughest objections and obstacles to faith in Christ (p. 147)."

The most likely thing to prevent this from happening is a group or table leader who thinks he is supposed to teach.

Read page 146 again. Explain the idea of listening in your own words.

_____

_____

_____

_____

_____

_____

Remember, your table leaders and helpers are facilitating an open discussion. They're using questions to give people direction and context to discover answers. This is a guided discussion; not a free for all. Also, the table leaders are not teaching information or telling people what the correct answer is. If you see some on your team fall into the "teaching trap," gently remind them they are facilitators, not teachers.

The most authentic way we can give them needed space is to realize that we also, still, carry unbelief within us. I fully believe in and trust in Jesus, yet I still struggle to believe I can do everything through Christ, who gives me strength (Philippians 4:13). I am much prone towards the state of the father with a demon possessed boy who was begging Jesus to heal his son in Mark 9:20-25, saying, *"Help me overcome my unbelief!"* When we are willing to face, and state, our unbelief it gives both permission and courage for others to face their unbelief as well. This creates an atmosphere for authentic faith sharing.

Facilitate Captivating Interactions

This is an intimidating chapter. If you read it and wanted to run the other way from a seeker group, I don't blame you. The skill to generate a great seeker group from scratch is an advanced skill. It takes someone who is experienced in leading groups to do this well. We're using the Sycamore Series so you don't have to develop your own content. This will let you concentrate on the most important leadership skills at this point: inviting seekers and leading your team.

Poole emphasizes the crucial role of the Bible in a seeker group. Many seekers, though, don't believe the Bible the same way you and I do. First, they probably do not know what the Bible is and they may not have a Bible of their own. Have a supply of Bibles at the start of the group to give to everybody. By giving everyone a Bible, you avoid embarrassing someone who doesn't own one. I recommend the New Living Translation for seekers because it is easy to read and understand.[8] Giving the same version to everyone will make things easier on those whose only copy of the Bible is a King James Version given to them by a significant person.

More specific instructions on how to give out Bibles are given below.

Sharing Faith Takes a Village

Growing up in the 1960s and 1970s, I was taught that the highest form of evangelism was the personal Bible study. The goal was to talk to someone and invite him to a one-on-one Bible study. This led us to do cold turkey door knocking. I remember it well.

"Excuse me, Ma'am. We're doing a back to the Bible campaign and we'd like to study the Bible with you." Then, wham! The door would be slammed shut. It was tough, but that's what we did.

You may think this is the kind of evangelism we've been leading up to all along. It's not. In fact, I seldom do personal Bible studies anymore.

Individual Bible studies don't seem to be as effective now. People are not very responsive to a canned, "guide me down your list of scriptures" approach. I certainly do engage in conversation with individuals about faith, Jesus, the Bible, etc. But these conversations tend to be more in the form of asking one another questions.

When a person did become a believer through personal Bible study, they became highly attached to me for up to the next two years! I truly became their parent (this is not bad in and of itself. Paul called Timothy *"my dear son"* in 2 Timothy 2:1). The problem was I could only have five or six of these intense relationships at any given time. That limited the number of people I could talk with about Jesus.

In our mission work in Africa we discovered that people like to come to faith with others who are doing the same thing. This was such a freeing discovery. Now, rather than me carrying all the weight, I only had to provide the opportunity to explore faith in Jesus. The seekers mostly taught themselves. When we came back to the U.S. I discovered the same thing was true here. The idea that people prefer to explore faith with others who are doing the same thing has revolutionized my thinking and practice. Now I can work with six, eight, or even twelve or more seekers at the same time, and, rather than forming their identity around me, they form their identity around their group. They become a "band of brothers (and sisters)."

Comparing Conversion Patterns

8. You can order the *New Living Translation* paperback from Bible.com for $4 each.

What makes coming to faith in groups the more productive avenue now? George Hunter III, in his book *The Celtic Way of Evangelism*, compares two historical conversion patterns that he calls the Roman and the Celtic patterns.[9] The Roman pattern is typical of what we today might call the "modern" conversion pattern while the Celtic pattern we would call "post-modern."

These two patterns are illustrated below. In the modern pattern (in which truth is embodied in information), we provide information which leads to a mental consent of faith on the part of the unbeliever. When faith exists, conversion follows, at which time the new believer is inducted into the community of faith.

In the post-modern conversion pattern the seeker begins with experience in the community. Because of their experience, they begin to address faith which leads to questions that can be answered with small pieces of information. In this pattern, conversion is something that grows and develops as more questions are asked and new information is considered.

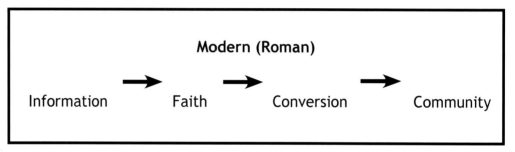

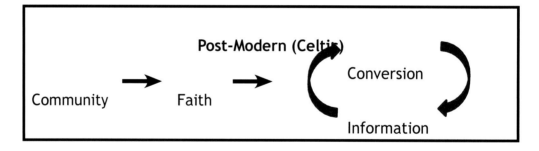

There are three critical assumptions made in these two conversion patterns.

Assumption 1—Truth

In the modern pattern truth is normative and held in substantially equal regard by both the believer and the unbeliever. This provides a starting point held in common. In the modern, Western World this starting point was that truth did exist in some knowable, universal form. What was disputed was how to pursue knowing that truth, whether by scientific enquiry or receiving divine communication.

In the post-modern pattern, truth is relative. The individual pos-

9. George Hunter, III, *The Celtic Way of Evangelism* (Nashville: Abingdon, 2000), 53.

sesses his own understanding of truth, but does not expect the other to share his views. Thus the believer and unbeliever begin at very different points. They can only begin the process of conversion by establishing and working on the same questions.

IN A POST-MODERN CONTEXT WE CAN ONLY BEGIN THE PROCESS OF CONVERSION BY WORKING ON THE SAME QUESTIONS.

Assumption 2—Process

In the modern pattern conversion is largely an intellectual process. The key question people wanted an answer for was, "Is it true?" In the modern American culture of 1960 through the mid-1980s, apologetics was king. Books like Josh McDowell's *Evidence That Demands a Verdict* were not only popular, they were effective. The operating principle was to provide sufficient evidence so that any reasonable person would surely believe that Christianity was true.

In the post-modern pattern, conversion is largely an experiential process. The key question people want answered is, "Will this work for me?" They look for the evidence of experience. They watch how we are living as Christians. If it looks possible they try it out and consider the outcomes in their lives.

Assumption 3—Community

In the modern pattern, the community of faith is a closed community. Until a person is inducted into the community he or she is restricted from participation in many of the community's activities and rituals. In my church background that meant no one was to be involved in a public role in the corporate worship service unless they were a baptized believer. Every now and then someone would slip through the screening process. The results could be messy.

In the post-modern pattern, the faith community is open. Seekers are invited into community to experience faith in life. Participation in community activities and rituals is offered. Tracy Balzer describes how Celtic Christians invited pagan seekers into the midst of their communities of faith and offer them an *anamchara*, a soul-friend. "The *anamchara* was one who would recognize the image of God in each person, treating each seeker as he would treat Christ himself, creating a haven where truth could be spoken in love."[10]

Inviting Guests for Your Group

At our Kairos kick-off event in 2005 we gathered over seventy leaders of significant, regional churches from Churches of Christ across America for what we called the St. Louis Summit. We invited Thom Rainer to speak to this group of leaders about his research findings on faith in America.

Thom challenged us with the following statistics about his findings

10. Tracy Balzer, *Thin Places* (Siloam Springs, AR: Leafwood, 2007), 50.

from the Unchurched:

- Over 80% of the Unchurched people Thom's team interviewed said they would come to church if a Christian invited them.

- Over 80% also said they had never been invited to church.

But someone saying they would come and then actually coming are two different things. So, Thom and his team asked them if they really would come. Here's what happened. Thom's research team went to all fifty states and invited people to go to specific churches with them.

- 80% said they would come if invited and someone went with them.

- 69% actually went when the person who invited them to church went with them.

- 12% went to church when they said but had to make the trip alone.

Watch the video clip of Thom's presentation at http://kairoschurch-planting.org/videos/thom-rainer-on-inviting-people-to-church/.[11]

Action Step: Inviting Seekers

Will you invite people who are not practicing believers to your group? Remember, the definition of a seeker group is that fifty percent or more of the people are not practicing Christians. Hopefully by this time you feel reasonably comfortable and confident to strike up a conversation where you invite people to join your seeker group. Remember what Thom Rainer said. Don't just tell them where and when. Give them a map and instructions. Call them during the week to tell them how excited you are and to let them know about some of the details. Then meet them and go together.

Recording

Complete Lesson 10 in your Personal Answer Book.

---

11. Thom Rainer video link: resources.kairoschurchplanting.org/modules/resources/?tac=45

Lesson 11
Your Seeker Group Meetings

People are amazing, interesting, and ever-changing. When we believers in Jesus learn to listen to people's faith journeys, we get to travel with them, by proxy, and become their guide. One of our planters once said, "I have learned to be consistently curious about people's lives."

I pray you will learn to be curious, too. Seeker group meetings are wonderful places to be curious about what God is doing in the lives of the people around us.

The Great Commission

John 20:21-23 The Lordship of Jesus

Again he said, "Peace be with you. As the Father has sent me, so I am sending you." Then he breathed on them and said, "Receive the Holy Spirit. If you forgive anyone's sins, they are forgiven. If you do not forgive them, they are not forgiven."

The deity and lordship of Jesus is the ultimate stumbling block to faith in our pluralistic context. It's acceptable to view Jesus as an exceptionally good person, an insightful teacher, or a positive religious leader. It's altogether different to live out of John 14:6 where Jesus says, *"I am the way, the truth, and the life. No one can come to the Father except through me."*

This exclusive claim of Christianity in general, and Jesus specifically, is the number one defeater belief Tim Keller heard from a survey of twenty-five year-old New Yorkers who were asked to complete the sentence, "Christianity cannot be true because of _____."

One of the main answers he heard from this group was the defeater belief of pluralism, which Keller describes in this way:[12]

No one should insist his or her view of God is better than all the rest. Every religion is an equally valid expression of spiritual reality. How dare Christians insist that their religion is the only one that is 'right' and true. Millions of people in other religions have had divine, spiritual encounters. They have built marvelous civilizations, many that pre-date Christianity, and have had their lives and characters changed by their experience of faith. The claim of Christianity that it is the only correct religion and all others are false takes one's breath away. And besides, it also appears to many to be a threat to international peace.[13]

One of the subtle ways in which pluralism works against Christian

---

12. Two good resources on pluralism are: Dennis L. Okholm and Timothy R. Phillips, *Four Views on Salvation in a Pluralistic World* (Grand Rapids, MI: Zondervan, 1995) and Ronald H. Nash, *Is Jesus the Only Savior?* (Grand Rapids, MI: Zondervan, 1994).

13. Keller, "Defeater Beliefs," 3.

faith is the erosion of the acceptance of the lordship of Jesus. There is a growing unease even among many Christians to claim Jesus as Lord. To say he is Lord implies that other choices are incorrect. Research by Ed Stetzer showed:

- 57% of people ages 20-29 believe that there is only one God and he is described in the Bible.

But his research also showed that:

- 58% believe the God of the Bible is no different from the gods or spiritual beings depicted by world religions such as Islam, Hinduism, Buddhism, etc.[14]

At face value these numbers don't add up, at least if it is the same group of people saying they both believe there is only one God but that the God of the Bible is no different from other spiritual beings. That is perhaps the point. In our pluralist, relative world people are fairly comfortable holding as true two ideas that would appear mutually exclusive. As you listen to others, how do you hear them finishing this sentence? "Christianity cannot be true because _____."

Believing Jesus is Lord

What is this mission upon which the Lord Jesus sends his disciples and how are the waiting children of God to appropriately accept God's missional invitation?

Believing in Jesus is the sole requirement (John 1:12; 3:16; 20:30-31). The compelling message of John is that there is no other god than this one, seen in Jesus as *"the way and the truth and the life"* (14:6). Anyone who has not made this confession is urged, implored, begged to believe in Jesus because *"Whoever believes in the Son has eternal life, but whoever rejects the Son will not see life, for God's wrath remains on them"* (John 3:36).

The response of those who hear the message decides whether their sins are forgiven or retained. The disciples are to provide witness and content to the lordship of Jesus while God acts based on the acceptance or rejection of Jesus as Savior.

J. Marsh responds to John's commission by saying, "But though this sounds stern and harsh, it is simply the result of the preaching of the gospel, which either brings men to repent as they hear of the ready and costly forgiveness of God, or leaves them unresponsive to the offer of forgiveness which is the gospel, and so they are left in their sins."[15]

There is no other alternative. One either accepts Jesus as Lord and surrenders complete allegiance to him or rejects Jesus and walks away into the darkness of the kingdom of the prince of this world.

---

14. Ed Stetzer, *Lost and Found: The Younger Unchurched and the Churches That Reach Them* (Nashville: B&H, 2009).

15. J. Marsh, *The Gospel of St. John* (New York: Penguin, 1968), 641-642.

How would you explain the idea of "Jesus is Lord" to someone in our highly pluralist world?

_____

_____

_____

_____

Reading: Poole, Chapters 8-10

There are a few key ideas in these final three chapters to prepare you to conduct seeker groups.

First, you will need to connect with your seeker friends outside of the group (Poole, 209). As the group leader you need to contact each of your guests other than at group. The week after your first Sycamore meeting call each person/couple. During that call express your delight that they were at the group and your anticipation to see them again at the next meeting. Between the fourth and fifth meetings, call them to say thank you for coming. Ask them what they are thinking about their faith journey during the group. Let them talk, then ask them how they are feeling. See how useful these two questions are! Finally, ask if there is anything you can specifically pray for them about. No matter if they tell you anything or not, pray for them over the phone right then. Make it a simple, direct, short prayer. Act like this is a normal thing to do.

Second, train your group helpers. The people you have recruited to help you are a team. You are the team leader. You are casting the vision for a seeker group. You are building the desire in their hearts to connect with lost people. You are teaching them to be evangelistic bringers. And you are training them to be good table leaders. That's a lot! This is leadership. On page 215 Poole gives a checklist of items for you to keep in mind as you train your team. There is more on training in the strategic assignment section.

Right now, stop and pray for your team. Send an email or call your prayer team to let them know what is happening in the seeker group. Ask them to pray for your group helpers and seekers.

Third, prepare to lead seekers across the line of faith.

In sharing faith, we need to recognize the point of when to address the big question, "What do you think of Jesus?" and its corollary, "How are you going to respond to him?" The second biggest task of this module is to address these questions with each of your guests.

When you complete your seeker group, meet with each of your guests. If they came as a couple, meet with them as a couple. If they are single and the same gender as you, meet with them as a singles. If they are the opposite gender, be sure to take your spouse or a friend along.

The purpose of this meeting is to ask your guest if there are any questions they are working on that you can help them with. Don't work on any questions that arise right then unless they are simple. Set up another time to focus on the bigger questions (this is part of providing next step opportunities) or invite your guest to another group. During this conversation, pull out a copy of *Your Spiritual Journey Guide*. Go over that with them just as we talked about earlier. For couples, have both the man and woman mark where they are on the guide. If one or both of them is getting close to Jesus, ask, "Do you think you are ready to believe in Jesus and become one of his followers?" That's the big question. If they respond with yes ask them if they know what that entails. Then you can talk about confessing Jesus and baptism.

If they say no, go back to *Your Spiritual Journey Guide*. Ask them where they see themselves now, where they'd like to be in 6 months, and how you can help them get there.

Funnel of Consideration

A seeker group is part of a process that unchurched people move through as they consider faith in Jesus. The picture in the sidebar illustrates this process. I call it the "funnel of consideration."

The funnel of consideration is predicated on the understanding that God is actively seeking his people and that he provides opportunity and circumstances that reveal his presence. This is the central theme of the *Missio Dei*. New Christians experience God's active seeking in their lives. We often hear new Christians say that one of the critical moments of their faith development occurred when they realized God was pursuing them through their life, even when they were unaware.

Funnel of Consideration

Meeting Points

Points of Entry

Sharing Events

Discipling

What does the funnel of consideration do? It illustrates the pathway that people follow towards faith. It's a map. Let's follow its path. Someone who is not a believer exists outside the funnel. Somewhere, somehow the unbeliever meets a Christian. This is a meeting point. We could rely on random meetings and hope that everyone involved realizes what God is doing. But the funnel reminds us that meeting points do not have to be random; we can plan them.

Meeting Points

What turns an event into a meeting point? First, an event becomes a meeting point when we believers make a confession of our faith. We can do this in as simple a way as putting out a sign, handing out a card with our church website, or praying for the other person on the spot. Let's say your church is doing a park clean up as servant evangelism. What do people see who are driving by or walking in the park? They see a group of people doing something good, but that's all. Unless they ask or you deliberately go tell them they have no idea who you are or why you are doing this. If you put up a sign that says, "Cleaned by Friendly Church" you have made a confession of faith, turning a random event into a meeting point.

An event also becomes a meeting point when you give people the opportunity to respond by providing you their contact information. For example, one church planter set up a water bottle give away booth at their neighborhood association's National Night Out safety event. They also did a movie ticket raffle. If you signed up for the raffle—your name, cell phone number, and email—you had the chance to win a $25 movie ticket. With a $25 investment, the planter gained the names of over sixty people who voluntarily gave permission to help them learn a little bit more about Jesus.

National Night Out

Point of Entry Event

The Point of Entry event is similar to a meeting point, but it adds one more characteristic. Point of Entry events let you deliberately and powerfully share your faith story. A church planter did a "Bible Fair" in the park each summer as his Point of Entry event. The Bible Fair lasted three half-days. The church set up booths for games, crafts, Bible story time, face painting, singing, and other activities that churches do at Vacation Bible Schools. Parents brought their children to the park, registered them (that's how you gather their contact information), and then walked them around the activities. The planter added an adult story time where parents could hear a presentation about the church that was serving their children. This church grew by more than a hundred people each summer for several years through this one Point of Entry event.

Sharing Event

The Sharing Event answers the question, "When do people consider the claims of Jesus on their lives?" That's what a seeker group does. Where the Meeting Point and Point of Entry events tend to be one off events, the Sharing Event has multiple meetings. Its primary purpose is to let people encounter Jesus so they can make a reasonable decision about following him.

Your seeker group moves people down the funnel of consideration to the point of the Sharing Event. Here they will have the opportunity to really think about Jesus and his claim for their lives in a safe context with other people who are doing the same thing.

Action Step

Look at your church. Does it have an active funnel of consideration? On the bottom of this page, draw a funnel of consideration for your church. Write the names of ministries that could be used at each point of the funnel. When you are done, share this idea with one of your church leaders.

Recording

Transfer your Funnel of Consideration to Lesson 11 in your Personal Answer Book.

Missional Director Meeting

Get together with your missional director for meeting #4.

Lesson 12: Conduct a Seeker Group

This module is meant to help you become comfortable and practiced in sharing your faith with other people. The only way that more people will come to know the love and grace of God, the forgiveness of their sins through Jesus' blood, and the empowering, sustaining presence of the Holy Spirit in their lives, is through God's people. This is God's mission. It is ours as well.

As you worked through this workbook you did a lot of activities in which you shared your faith with other people. This makes you an expert in your church on sharing faith. Imagine that!

With this strategy assignment I want you to move beyond sharing your own faith. Here you will become a leader who knows how to help others share their faith too.

Your strategy assignment for this module is to plan and conduct a five-week seeker group using the *Sycamore Encounter Series* from Let's Start Talking. Order the following materials from FriendSpeak.org.

❑ Sycamore Training DVD, $19.99

❑ Sycamore Series #1 *The Life*, enough copies for everyone. These are sold in packs of 5 books for $25 plus shipping.

This material will walk you through what you need to know and do to accomplish this project. If you run into questions that are not answered here, ask your missional director for help. This is not rocket science. It is simply providing seekers a safe place, good material, and a lot of hospitality.

Enjoy!

Recording

Fill out Lesson 12 in your personal answer book as you work through these next few pages.

Your Team

Ask two other couples, or a total of four people, to join with you to run your seeker group. You're asking them for these four things:

1. Commit to eight weeks of gatherings, three for training and inviting and five weeks for the seeker group meetings.

2. Pray over guests the group will invite.

3. Invite those people to attend until you have at least eight people committed to coming.

4. Be good table leaders and helpers during the seeker group.

You also need to ask someone to host the seeker group meetings in their home and someone else to provide childcare (see below).

Training Your Team

The key responsibilities for your team are:

• To be evangelistic bringers who invite guests to the group

• To pray for those on the invitation list and those who come

• To act as table leaders and helpers

If your team does these three tasks well, you will have a great group.

Table Leaders

Table leaders are responsible for facilitating discussion in their table groups by creating a safe, open atmosphere where guests feel free to ask honest questions about the Christian faith. They do not need to be experts or experienced teachers. They do need to be interested in introducing people to Jesus, willing to be evangelistic bringers, nonjudgmental, and willing to serve.

Table Helpers

Table helpers are responsible for helping the table leader create a safe, welcoming atmosphere for asking questions about the Christian faith. They need to be sensitive, nonjudgmental, willing to listen well and to serve.

Team Expectations

1. Attend all eight weeks: three weeks for training and inviting and five weeks of group seeker meetings

2. Read *The Life* book

3. Invite and bring guests with them to the group

4. Prepare for each group time by praying for the guests and reviewing the week's material

5. Be sensitive to the spiritual and emotional needs of guests

The Training Process

You will do three weeks of training together.

Week 1: Overview

During the overview week you will introduce your team to the Sycamore Series *#1 The Life* material. Have books for everyone and hand them out. Let people look at them. Explain to them what you have been doing in the Emerging Leader Training series and, particularly, in the *Sharing Faith* module. Share your motivations, your hopes, and your struggles. This is part of learning how to cast vision as a leader.

Talk them through the purpose of a seeker group.

- Define what a seeker group is.

- Describe what a group meeting will be like.

- State the goal: to provide people the opportunity to meet Jesus and consider his claims on their lives.

With that background in place, get out your calendars. Make sure everyone is able to be at every group meeting. If you need to make a calendar adjustment, now is the time to do it.

What if it's not possible for someone to be at every meeting? Use your best judgment. Recognize that life does happen and do the best you can to provide the best experience for those people who will be your guests.

Now comes the most important part of the evening. Put a large sheet of paper on the wall or on an easel. Make a list of the people the team will commit to invite. You have a list of twenty people in your Personal Answer Book to start you off. Help your team brainstorm their own guest lists.

Talk through your strategy for inviting guests.

- Assign a team member to invite each person on the list.

- Put two dates on the paper. These are commitment dates. The first date you will see how many people have been invited and what their responses are. The second date is the final date by which every person on your list should have been invited in person (or in a phone conversation). Emails, Twitter, Facebook, etc. do not constitute an invitation, though they can be an encouragement.

- Prepare a printed invitation to give to the people you are inviting. Be sure it includes the specifics of when, what, where, and what time. Tell them childcare will be provided along with refreshments. If someone in your group is great with computer graphics let them take on this task.

- Finish your evening in prayer over these names. Plan to make this a climactic act. Share scripture together. Turn a spotlight on the names and turn down the other lights. Gather everyone around the paper to put hands on it. Do one of these suggestions or something else to raise the group's awareness that God is using them to do something amazing and holy.

Week 2: Training

Your team will watch and talk through the Sycamore Training DVD to learn how to be table leaders and helpers for a seeker group. The DVD is divided into multiple sections. Watch a section then pause to talk about it. What were the key points? How do you see this working? There is a DVD training guide available for $7.95 if you feel that will help you get the most out of your training evening.

Remember to pray over your invitees again. If this is the date you chose for your mid-point check up on invitations, light a fire under your team!

Week 3: Model Evening

At this final training meeting, you will run your group through the first unit. Do everything just like you will for the five seeker group weeks. Meet at your host house. This will let you see and feel what your group meeting will be like. Share with your host what you have been doing. Go over the list of people you have been inviting. Since your group is small this week, use just one table. Everyone bring your *Life* books and your Bibles. Wear nametags. Tell your joke. Have refreshments. Sit at your table. As you go through this practice run, identify things you need to iron out before the real thing begins.

Meeting Preparation

The best meeting place for a small seeker group is in someone's home. There are positives and negatives to a home meeting.

Strengths

- A home often is the most available venue.

- Many people find a home non-threatening.

- You can more easily control the environment.

Weaknesses

- A host needs to prepare and clean up.

- There may or may not be good childcare space.

- For some, a home is too personal.

For your seeker group plan to meet in a home. It is best if this is not your own home or any of your team couples' homes. Ask someone in your church to host your seeker group. There should be someone who loves hosting and is gifted at it. Provide them an opportunity for evangelistic service. Their home does not have to be fancy. It does need to be clean, comfortable and with adequate lighting.

Host Preparation

- Open their home up for six weeks of meetings (one model meeting and five group meetings).

- Be warm and hospitable.

- Have sufficient room for two table groups.

- Have a childcare space that is separate from your meeting space.

- Provide the equipment and materials for serving coffee and tea (see refreshment list below).

Your Pre-meeting Preparation

- Provide an accurate map and address to all guests.

- Turn on the porch light and interior lights.

- Place name tags in the entry area.

- Bring your hostess flowers for the evening. (It's a nice touch and a good thank you.)

- Arrange tables and chairs for your table groups.

- Provide space to hang coats and keep other personal items.

- Adjust the temperature so it will be comfortable.

Childcare

If no one on your team or your guests has young children then you don't need to worry with childcare. However, that is unlikely. Since childcare is so costly, if you want people to come, you need to provide childcare.

Childcare is a volunteer position. Who at your church is gifted and experienced with children? This could be someone in your church's children's ministry or an experienced, trusted older teen.

The childcare provider's job will be to take the children for the entire meeting time. When your guests arrive, spend part of the first 15 minutes getting the children settled into their space for the evening. An experienced childcare provider will know what to do, how to entertain, and even teach the children. A five-week group of Bible units for the children would be perfect.

Refreshments

People talk more easily over refreshments. That's the rule. Each meeting your host should prepare coffee (decaf and regular) and hot water for tea. The host is also responsible for providing cream and sugar, plates, cups, and silverware.

Organize your snacks/desserts ahead of time for the first two weeks. Week one of your group meetings the snacks should be prepared by the host. During your opening time, as you give instructions for the refreshments, mention that next week so-and-so is providing _____ for next week. Then let the group know that bringing snacks/desserts is something that will be planned each week for the following week. If someone wants to share in this hospitality they are very welcome to do so.

You may be wondering why you would ask guests to provide something. The answer is: you don't want them to always feel like guests. You want them to feel like they are part of the group. Offering to let them provide food is a built in way to do this.

Don't forget the children! They will need appropriate drinks and snacks too.

Schedule

Feel free to adjust the times of this suggested schedule to meet the needs of your group. When we first started doing the Alpha Course we planned to meet for supper and group meeting during the week. We found during our practice that our team could not get there in time! We changed to Sunday evenings and it worked great.

7:00-7:15 Arrive and greet

Set up a nametag table close to the entry door. Station one person there to greet each person and direct them to prepare a name tag.

7:15-7:30 Informal welcome and snack

Gain attention and gather everyone together for welcome.

- Give the welcome.
- Provide instructions for the evening. You might say something like, "Help yourselves to something to eat and drink. Feel free to mingle. We'll gather all together again here at 7:30."
- Say a short prayer of thanks.

Note: sharing food together is a critical point of hospitality. It opens people up and prepares them to share.

7:30-8:30 Table groups

Table groups should hold six to eight people each. In many homes, your tables may be in different rooms. If that is the case, first gather everyone into the central room.

- Tell your joke and gather people's attention.

- Introduce the evening's topic.

- Send everyone to their tables with an invitation to take drinks and snacks with them.

In Your First Meeting

- **Introduce everyone.** A good icebreaker would be effective at this point. At its simplest, begin with yourself and say your name, tell where you live (neighborhood name), and one fact about yourself or your family. Then have each person do that. For couples, ask the second person in the couple to add another fact.

- **Introduce what you are doing.** We're going to look at who Jesus is. We'll be using a short guide to help us called The Sycamore Series. Hand out books to every person. Husbands and wives each get their own book. Since the Bible is our primary resource we've got Bibles for everyone too. Hand out the Bibles then go over the Bible Introduction. Our goal is to help each other look at Jesus. We want to be a group where we feel comfortable to ask our questions safely. There aren't any dumb questions. We all come with different backgrounds and experiences. We do want to respect everyone, speak with kindness, and be willing to share our thoughts and feelings about the topics.

- **Introduce the table leaders and helpers.** Assign tables. Keep couples together. You do not necessarily need to keep people together who are already friends, nor do inviters need to sit with those they invited. Use your best judgment. Tell people what time to stop. Send them to their tables.

8:30 End

Ask everyone to pick up around them, take dishes to the kitchen, etc. Try to get people out the door by 8:45 so your host can clean up.

Bible Introduction

When you hand out the Bibles take two minutes to give an overview. Here's an example of what you can say:

The Bible is not just one book. It is actually a collection of many books written by many different people over a long period of time. Yet what draws these books together is that they are part of one story: the story of a God who wants to have relationship with the people whom he made, but who so many times struggle to know him.

In our group over the next five weeks we're going to talk about Jesus. God said Jesus was his son. Jesus' story is in what is called the New Testament, in the back part of the Bible. The New Testament begins with four books called the gospels, which means "good news". These four "good news" books are titled Matthew, Mark, Luke, and John.

Matthew, Mark, Luke, and John were all followers of Jesus. Two of these men, Matthew and John, were part of the group of twelve men Jesus chose as apostles. The apostles lived with Jesus for three years, hearing him teach and watching him interact with all kinds of people. The other two men, Mark and Luke, were "second generation" followers of Jesus. Mark was a student of the apostle Peter. Luke was a student of the apostle Paul.

Let's look at Matthew on page _____. You'll notice that the page before Matthew says "New Testament." Then on the first page of Matthew it has a large number 1 followed by smaller numbers. We refer to the large numbers as chapters and the smaller numbers as verses. Matthew didn't write this book with chapters and verses; they were added later to help us find our place.

Also look at these section headings. In the first chapter of Matthew there are two: *The Ancestors of Jesus the Messiah* and *The Birth of Jesus the Messiah*. These headings were also added to help us keep track of what is happening.

Outside Calls

The goal of a seeker group is to help people meet Jesus and consider his claims upon their life. You, as the facilitator and organizer of the group, accept the responsibility to follow through on this purpose. The only way you can do this is to talk with your guests personally. Below is your schedule for making these calls:

❑ **First Group Meeting, Week 4.** Make the first personal phone call to each couple and single.

- Thank them for coming. Tell them how good it was to meet them.

- Ask if there is anything you can do for them.

- Tell them you look forward to seeing them next week.

❑ **Fourth Group Meeting, Week 7.** Make the second personal phone call to each couple and single.

- Thank them for coming.

- Ask if there is anything you can do for them.

- Remind them that next week is the last week. Mention that you have a gift you are looking forward to giving them.

❑ Within two weeks after the final meeting, have a face-to-face meeting with each couple or single.

- Take them out to coffee.

- Ask them if there are any questions they are working on that you can help them with.

- Go through *Your Spiritual Journey Guide* with them.

The Gift

The Ultimate Gift is a great movie about an extremely wealthy grandfather who wants to give his grown, and spoiled brat, grandson the ultimate gift. In a very real sense that is what you want to give to your guests. You would like each of them to accept God's gift of grace, through Jesus, and sealed by the Holy Spirit. There is nothing else you could do or say that could come close to this gift.

Whether or not the seekers in your group choose to accept God's gift of grace at this point, you need to offer them another kind of gift, one of remembrance. At the final meeting, present every family or person a small, standard-sized picture of your group in a frame. This means, of course, that meeting four will be your picture-taking meeting. Make a big deal of it at meeting three. Talk about where you will take it, what kind of clothes you want to wear, etc. Let people feel special about it. To increase that special feeling ask someone in your church who is a good photographer to come take the picture for you.

This one small gift will help you build momentum in your group. It gives you a way to encourage people to keep coming. And it is another show of hospitality at the end of your group.

Missional Director Meeting

As you conclude your seeker group, be sure to talk with your missional director about your experience.

What's Next?

My prayer is that your seeker group will be a fantastic experience. We don't know the outcomes yet, but we do know God is at work. So what happens next?

One of the principles you need to learn when working with people is to always plan for the next step. By the time your group has been together five weeks there may be a good seed for doing another group. The Sycamore Series has three unit books. You might choose to complete the series.

Another option I would suggest is the Alpha Course. I've mentioned it at places in this workbook. Alpha is a ten-week video based introduction to Christianity. It is more complicated to do than your seeker group. If you are interested in Alpha for your church, I suggest you go to alphusa. org and look at the various training opportunities that are available. Better yet, search for an Alpha course near you and go through it. The Alpha people also run regional and national training events that are very good.

Thank you for your interest and commitment in learning how to share your faith with God's lost people around you. May He bless you with attractive peace and winsome ways.

Selected Bibliography

Balzer, Tracy. *Thin Places*, Siloam Springs, AR: Leafwood, 2007.

Banks, William L. *In Search of the Great Commission: What Did Jesus Really Say?* Chicago: Moody, 1991.

Bauckham, Richard. *God Crucified: Monotheism and Christology in the New Testament*, Grand Rapids: Eerdmans, 1998.

Bayer, Charles H. *A Resurrected Church: Christianity After the Death of Christendom*, Chalice Press, 2001.

Beasley-Murray, G. R. B*aptism in the New Testament*, Grand Rapids, MI: Eerdmans, 1962.

Brownson, James V. *The Promise of Baptism: An Introduction to Baptism in Scripture and the Reformed Tradition*, Grand Rapids, MI: Eerdmans, 2007.

Butterfield, Rosaria. *Secret Thoughts of an Unlikely Convert*, Kindle edition, Crown & Covenant, 2012.

Cecil, Douglas M. *The 7 Principles of an Evangelistic Life*, Chicago: Moody, 2003, p. 174.

Clinton, Robert J. *Leadership Emergence Theory*, Altadena, CA: Barnabas Resources, 1989.

Eswine, Zack. *Preaching to a Post-Everything World*, Grand Rapids: Baker, 2008.

Galli, Mark. *Francis of Assisi and His World*, InterVarsity, 2003.

Green, Michael. *Evangelism in the Early Church*, Grand Rapids, MI: Eerdmans, 1970, 2003.

Hicks, John Mark & Greg Taylor, *Down in the River to Pray*, Siloam Springs, AR: Leafwood, 2004.

Hunter, George III, *The Celtic Way of Evangelism*, Nashville: Abingdon, 2000.

Hybels & Mittelberg, *Becoming a Contagious Christian*, Kindle Edition, p. 46.

Keller, Tim. *Redeemer Church Planting Manual*, New York: Redeemer Church Planting Center, 2002.

Kinnamon, David & Gabe Lyons, *unChristian: What a New Generation Really Thinks about Christianity...and Why It Matters*, Baker, 2007.

Kostenberger, Andreas J. *A Theology of John's Gospel and Letters*, Grand Rapids, MI: Zondervan, 2009.

Lamott, Anne. *Traveling Mercies*, New York: Anchor, 2000.

Lewis, C.S. *Surprised by Joy: The Shape of My Early Lif,*. Houghton Mifflin Harcourt, revised ed., 1995.

Marsh, J. *The Gospel of St. John*, Penguin, 1968.

McGavran, Donald G. *Understanding Church Growth*, Grand Rapids, MI: Zondervan, 1960.

Nash, Ronald H. *Is Jesus the Only Savior?* Grand Rapids, MI: Zondervan, 1994.

Okholm, Dennis L. & Timothy R. Phillips. *Four Views on Salvation in a Pluralistic World*, Grand Rapids, MI: Zondervan, 1995.

Olds, Jacqueline & Richard S. Schwartz. *The Lonely American: Drifting Apart in the Twenty First Century*, Boston, Beacon, 2009.

Quick, O. C. *The Christian Sacraments*, London, 2nd ed, 1932.

Rainer, Thom. *Surprising Insights from the Unchurched and Proven Ways to Reach Them*, Zondervan, 2001.

Rainer, Thom & Jess. *The Millennials*, B&H Publishing, 2010.

Rambo, Lewis. *Understanding Religious Conversion*, New Haven, CT: Yale University Press, 1993.

Rohrmayer, Gary. *FirstSteps for Planting a Missional Church*, Your Journey Resources, 2006.

Rusaw, Rick & Eric Swanson, *The Externally Focused Church*, Loveland, CO: Group, 2004.

Sayer, George. *Jack: A Life of C.S. Lewis*, Crossway, 2005.

Simpson, Michael L. *Permission Evangelism*, Colorado Springs, CO: NexGen, 2004.

Sjogren, Steve. *Conspiracy of Kindness, rev. ed.* Regal, 2008.

Stark, Rodney. *The Rise of Christianity*, Princeton: Princeton University Press, 1996.

Stetzer, Ed. *Lost and Found: The Younger Unchurched and the Churches That Reach Them*, Nashville: B&H, 2009.

Strobel, Lee. *The Case for Faith: A Journalist Investigates the Toughest Objections to Christianity*, Grand Rapids, MI: Zondervan, 2000.

Sylvia, Ron. *High Definition Church Planting*, Ocala, FL: High Definition Resources, 2006.

Thompson, David M. *Baptism, Church, and Society in Modern Britain*, Waynesboro, GA: Paternoster, 2005.

Webber, Robert. *Ancient-Future Evangelism: Making Your Church a Faith-Forming Community*, Grand Rapids, MI: Baker, 2003.

Witherington, Ben III. *Troubled Waters: Rethinking the Theology of Baptism*, Waco, TX: Baylor University Press, 2007.

Winner, Lauren. *Girl Meets God*, New York: Random House, 2003.

Wright,N. T. *Surprised by Hope*, New York: Harper One, 2008.

Wright, Christopher J.H. *The Mission of God: Unlocking the Bible's Grand Narrative*, Downers Grove, IL: InterVarsity Press, 2006.

Yeakley, Flavil. *Why Churches Grow*, Nashville: Christian Communications, 1979.

SEARCHING

FOLLOWING

NOT INTERESTED	CURIOUSLY SEEKING	ASSERTIVELY SEEKING	FAITH COMMITMENT	ACTIVELY FOLLOWING	GROWING IN FELLOWSHIP	MAKING AN IMPACT
• Aware but not interested • OK for you, but it's not for me. • Many misconceptions of Christianity • Negative view of Christianity and religion • Believe all religions are the same • Have an indifferent attitude toward spiritual issues	• Open to spirituality • Realize there is more to life than what they have already experienced. • Attend Christian events out of curiosity not because of need • Still struggle with negative image of Christianity • Questioning the belief that all religions lead to the same God	• Taking positive steps to find needed answers • Intellectually believe in God • Beginning to grasp the implications of Christ's claims • Understand the difference between Christianity and religion • Struggle with intellectualizing Christianity	• Have come to the realization that they are powerless to achieve God's favor and forgiveness • Believe that Jesus Christ is God and have received Him as their risen Lord and only Savior • Have made a decision to turn their lives and wills over to the care and control of Jesus Christ	• Have entered into a mentoring relationship with another Christian • Beginning to joyfully grasp the spiritual blessings in Christ and the core elements of following Jesus Christ as Lord • Share Christ naturally with others • Struggle with changing value system and assurance of salvation	• Growing in intimacy with God through prayer and Bible study • Growing in their relationships with fellow Christians through small group participation and service in the local church • Beginning to take hold of Biblical values • Discover not all Christians are growing.	• Deeply intimate with God and practicing spiritual renewal skills • Learning how to effectively share their faith • Mentoring others and being influential for Christ • Practicing financial stewardship • Ministering according to spiritual gifts and serving where needed
RESISTING	QUESTIONING	RESPONDING	EMBRACING	ADJUSTING	STABILIZING	REPRODUCING

114

SEARCHING

FOLLOWING

NOT INTERESTED

- Aware but not interested
- OK for you, but it's not for me.
- Many misconceptions of Christianity
- Negative view of Christianity and religion.
- Believe all religions are the same
- Have an indifferent attitude toward spiritual issues.

RESISTING

CURIOUSLY SEEKING

- Open to spirituality
- Realize there is more to life than what they have already experienced.
- Attend Christian events out of curiosity not because of need.
- Still struggle with negative image of Christianity
- Questioning the belief that all religions lead to the same God

QUESTIONING

ASSERTIVELY SEEKING

- Taking positive steps to find needed answers
- Intellectually believe in God
- Beginning to grasp the implications of Christ's claims
- Understand the difference between Christianity and religion
- Struggle with intellectualizing Christianity

RESPONDING

FAITH COMMITMENT

- Have come to the realization that they are powerless to achieve God's favor and forgiveness
- Believe that Jesus Christ is God and have received Him as their risen Lord and only Savior
- Have made a decision to turn their lives and wills over to the care and control of Jesus Christ

EMBRACING

ACTIVELY FOLLOWING

- Have entered into a mentoring relationship with another Christian
- Beginning to joyfully grasp the spiritual blessings in Christ and the core elements of following Jesus Christ as Lord
- Share Christ naturally with others
- Struggle with changing value system and assurance of salvation

ADJUSTING

GROWING IN FELLOWSHIP

- Growing in intimacy with God through prayer and Bible study
- Growing in their relationships with fellow Christians through small group participation and service in the local church
- Beginning to take hold of Biblical values.
- Discover not all Christians are growing.

STABILIZING

MAKING AN IMPACT

- Deeply intimate with God and practicing spiritual renewal skills.
- Learning how to effectively share their faith
- Mentoring others and being influential for Christ
- Practicing financial stewardship
- Ministering according to spiritual gifts and serving where needed

REPRODUCING

SEARCHING

FOLLOWING

NOT INTERESTED

- Aware but not interested.
- OK for you, but it's not for me.
- Many misconceptions of Christianity.
- Negative view of Christianity and religion.
- Believe all religions are the same.
- Have an indifferent attitude toward spiritual issues.

RESISTING

CURIOUSLY SEEKING

- Open to spirituality.
- Realize there is more to life than what they have already experienced.
- Attend Christian events out of curiosity, not because of need.
- Still struggle with negative image of Christianity.
- Questioning the belief that all religions lead to the same God.

QUESTIONING

ASSERTIVELY SEEKING

- Taking positive steps to find needed answers.
- Intellectually believe in God.
- Beginning to grasp the implications of Christ's claims.
- Understand the difference between Christianity and religion.
- Struggle with intellectualizing Christianity.

RESPONDING

FAITH COMMITMENT

- Have come to the realization that they are powerless to achieve God's favor and forgiveness.
- Believe that Jesus Christ is God and have received Him as their risen Lord and only Savior.
- Have made a decision to turn their lives and wills over to the care and control of Jesus Christ.

EMBRACING

ACTIVELY FOLLOWING

- Have entered into a mentoring relationship with another Christian.
- Beginning to joyfully grasp the spiritual blessings in Christ and the core elements of following Jesus Christ as Lord.
- Share Christ naturally with others.
- Struggle with changing value system and assurance of salvation.

ADJUSTING

GROWING IN FELLOWSHIP

- Growing in intimacy with God through prayer and Bible study.
- Growing in their relationships with fellow Christians through small group participation and service in the local church.
- Beginning to take hold of Biblical values.
- Discover not all Christians are growing.

STABILIZING

MAKING AN IMPACT

- Deeply intimate with God and practicing spiritual renewal skills.
- Learning how to effectively share their faith.
- Mentoring others and being influential for Christ.
- Practicing financial stewardship.
- Ministering according to spiritual gifts and serving where needed.

REPRODUCING

SEARCHING

NOT INTERESTED

- Aware but not interested.
- OK for you, but it's not for me.
- Many misconceptions of Christianity.
- Negative view of Christianity and religion.
- Believe all religions are the same.
- Have an indifferent attitude toward spiritual issues.

RESISTING

QUESTIONING

CURIOUSLY SEEKING

- Open to spirituality.
- Realize there is more to life than what they have already experienced.
- Attend Christian events out of curiosity, not because of need.
- Still struggle with negative image of Christianity.
- Questioning the belief that all religions lead to the same God.

RESPONDING

ASSERTIVELY SEEKING

- Taking positive steps to find needed answers.
- Intellectually believe in God.
- Beginning to grasp the implications of Christ's claims.
- Understand the difference between Christianity and religion.
- Struggle with intellectualizing Christianity.

FOLLOWING

FAITH COMMITMENT

- Have come to the realization that they are powerless to achieve God's favor and forgiveness.
- Believe that Jesus Christ is God and have received Him as their risen Lord and only Savior.
- Have made a decision to turn their lives and wills over to the care and control of Jesus Christ.

EMBRACING

ACTIVELY FOLLOWING

- Have entered into a mentoring relationship with another Christian.
- Beginning to joyfully grasp the spiritual blessings in Christ and the core elements of following Jesus Christ as Lord.
- Share Christ naturally with others.
- Struggle with changing value system and assurance of salvation.

ADJUSTING

GROWING IN FELLOWSHIP

- Growing in intimacy with God through prayer and Bible study.
- Growing in their relationships with fellow Christians through small group participation and service in the local church.
- Beginning to take hold of Biblical values.
- Discover not all Christians are growing.

STABILIZING

MAKING AN IMPACT

- Deeply intimate with God and practicing spiritual renewal skills.
- Learning how to effectively share their faith.
- Mentoring others and being influential for Christ.
- Practicing financial stewardship.
- Ministering according to spiritual gifts and serving where needed.

REPRODUCING

SEARCHING

FOLLOWING

NOT INTERESTED

- Aware but not interested.
- OK for you, but it's not for me.
- Many misconceptions of Christianity.
- Negative view of Christianity and religion.
- Believe all religions are the same.
- Have an indifferent attitude toward spiritual issues.

RESISTING

CURIOUSLY SEEKING

- Open to spirituality.
- Realize there is more to life than what they have already experienced.
- Attend Christian events out of curiosity, not because of need.
- Still struggle with negative image of Christianity.
- Questioning the belief that all religions lead to the same God.

QUESTIONING

ASSERTIVELY SEEKING

- Taking positive steps to find needed answers.
- Intellectually believe in God.
- Beginning to grasp the implications of Christ's claims.
- Understand the difference between Christianity and religion.
- Struggle with intellectualizing Christianity.

RESPONDING

FAITH COMMITMENT

- Have come to the realization that they are powerless to achieve God's favor and forgiveness.
- Believe that Jesus Christ is God and have received Him as their risen Lord and only Savior.
- Have made a decision to turn their lives and wills over to the care and control of Jesus Christ.

EMBRACING

ACTIVELY FOLLOWING

- Have entered into a mentoring relationship with another Christian.
- Beginning to joyfully grasp the spiritual blessings in Christ and the core elements of following Jesus Christ as Lord.
- Share Christ naturally with others.
- Struggle with changing value system and assurance of salvation.

ADJUSTING

GROWING IN FELLOWSHIP

- Growing in intimacy with God through prayer and Bible study.
- Growing in their relationships with fellow Christians through small group participation and service in the local church.
- Beginning to take hold of Biblical values.
- Discover not all Christians are growing.

STABILIZING

MAKING AN IMPACT

- Deeply intimate with God and practicing spiritual renewal skills.
- Learning how to effectively share their faith.
- Mentoring others and being influential for Christ.
- Practicing financial stewardship.
- Ministering according to spiritual gifts and serving where needed.

REPRODUCING

88516839R00075

Made in the USA
Middletown, DE
09 September 2018